Instant BRAINPOWER

Instant BRAINPOWER

BRIAN CLEGG

KOGAN PAGE

First South Asian Edition 2000

Kogan Page India Private Limited
4325/3 Ansari Road
New Delhi 110 002.

This edition is for sale in India, Bangladesh, Nepal, Pakistan and Sri Lanka only. Not for export elsewhere.

ISBN 81-7554-115-6

Published by Vinod Vasishtha for Kogan Page India Private Limited,
4325/3 Ansari Road, Daryaganj, New Delhi 110 002, and printed at
Rajkamal Electric Press, Delhi 110 033.

Contents

1 Brain bashing 1

Brainpower? 3
Meet your brain 3
Education – brain stretching, or brain deadening? 4
Knowledge, memory and creativity 4
Conscious and unconscious activity 5
Using this book 5

2 Getting the knowledge 7

What is knowledge? 9
The knowledge management business 10
A lot of theory 10
What about the Internet? 11
Becoming better knowledge managers 11

3 Memory 13

How memory works 15
Forgetting 15
Memory magic 16
The value of memory 17

4 Creativity 19

Creativity central 21
Born with it? 21
Other approaches 21
The creativity workout 22

5 The exercises 23

5.1 On the box 25
5.2 Water into wine 26
5.3 Broken record 28
5.4 Category magic 29
5.5 Doing and knowing 30
5.6 Metaphorically speaking 31
5.7 Sense and sensibility 32
5.8 Altered states 33
5.9 All that glisters 34
5.10 Chunks and breaks 35
5.11 Extremes 36
5.12 Surveying your mind 37
5.13 Story chains 38
5.14 Muddled model 39
5.15 One more time 40
5.16 Take a note 41
5.17 Words of wisdom 42
5.18 Round the world 43
5.19 Name game 44
5.20 Holistic awareness 45
5.21 Pub quiz 46
5.22 Number rhymes 47
5.23 No time to read 48
5.24 Spinning knowledge 49
5.25 Going down 50
5.26 The little black book 51
5.27 We ask the questions 52
5.28 Follow the finger 53
5.29 On the edge 54
5.30 Quick on the draw 55
5.31 Story time 56
5.32 Leaf mould 57
5.33 Car and goats 58
5.34 Found story 59
5.35 Remember, remember 60
5.36 Life saver 61
5.37 Get a laugh 62
5.38 Rapt concentration 63
5.39 Material gains 64
5.40 Twisters 65
5.41 Mapping for memory 66
5.42 Fact quest 67
5.43 Versatile coat hangers 68
5.44 Game theory 69

5.45	Technical creativity	70
5.46	Stolen thoughts	71
5.47	Broken CD	72
5.48	The bookshop raid	73
5.49	Birthday bonanza	74
5.50	Critical judgement	75
5.51	Number shapes	76
5.52	Encyclopedia dip	78
5.53	Horse whispers	79
5.54	Speed read	80
5.55	I never forget a face	81
5.56	The thrill factor	82
5.57	Different views	83
5.58	Binning paper	84
5.59	Something completely different	85
5.60	Programmed thought	86
5.61	Unconscious creativity	88
5.62	Scribbling	89
5.63	Questioning everything	90
5.64	Cloak and dagger	91
5.65	On the level	92
5.66	Go gallery	93
5.67	Strengthening your ghosts	94
5.68	School daze	95
5.69	Context is everything	96
5.70	Take a letter	97
5.71	Get another life	99
5.72	An excellent mistake	100
5.73	Using it	101

6 Other sources 103

More brain development	105
Web sources	105
Books	105

Appendix – The Selector 109

The Random selector	111
Techniques in timing order	112
Techniques in frequency order	113
Techniques in knowledge order	114
Techniques in memory order	115
Techniques in creativity order	116
Techniques in fun order	117

1

BRAIN BASHING

BRAINPOWER?

Instant Brainpower contains over 70 quick exercises which come together to provide a workout regime for the brain. Each exercise is short enough to fit it into a few spare minutes at any time of the day. As part of the Instant series (including *Instant Teamwork, Instant Creativity* and *Instant Time Management*), it is a handy resource for individuals, team leaders, managers and trainers.

The brain is our most important organ, yet we are given no instruction manual and very little training in using it. One of the biggest holes in our education is how to use our brains – it just doesn't appear in the curriculum (at least in the UK and the US – there is more effort made in Australia). Everyone's brain has much more capability than is ever used. From memory techniques to knowledge acquisition, this book gives your brain a chance to pump mental iron.

MEET YOUR BRAIN

You don't need to know a lot about the brain itself to use it more effectively, but a little background helps to put the rest into context. It's traditional to get rather excited about the brain, because the numbers involved are remarkable. A very basic model sees the brain as a set of simple switches – neurons – which, like a computer bit, can be in one of two states. However, given that the brain contains around 10 billion neurons, each capable of interacting with hundreds or thousands of others, the combinatorial explosion makes sure that simplicity doesn't enter into it. The numbers are dramatic. The dendrites that link the neurons amount to around 150,000 kilometres of wiring.

When you put the scale of the brain's capabilities against what it actually does, despite the immense complexity of the tasks it handles, there is no doubt that the brain is underworked. Estimates of the percentage usage vary from the conservative 10 per cent to as little as 0.1 per cent – whatever the true value, there is vast overcapacity.

It might seem reasonable that a particular part of the brain handles a particular function – in fact, this was the common understanding for many years – but sadly it isn't that simple. Even a basic brain function can result in action in many different areas. However, one way the brain is divided has value, even if it is only as a concept. For a long time it was argued that the left and right sides of the brain housed areas working in fundamentally different ways. The left was the cold, logical side. It was responsible for reasoning, language and maths. It handled tasks in a sequential, step-by-step manner. The right-hand side was the creative, arty side. It had a more parallel, holistic approach – hence it was particularly appropriate for pattern recognition and visual imagery. The right-hand side was the creative side whereas the left-hand side was the practical, down-to-earth side.

This theory is now in considerable doubt, but it leaves behind a valuable legacy. It may not be the left/right split that means our brains have two distinct modes of operation, but there is no doubt at all that they do. It may be, in fact, that the distinction is instead between the conscious (left brain) mind and the unconscious (right brain) – but whatever the cause, we (especially in the West) work most often in what can conveniently be referred to as left brain mode. To be creative in an applied way requires a flip-flop between the two modes – or even better a mix of the two. Left brain to assess the position, right brain to generate new ideas, left brain to assess the ideas, right brain to fix any problems… with a similar progression through implementation. Not only do we need practice in using our brains more efficiently, we also need practice in this creative flip and mix.

EDUCATION – BRAIN STRETCHING, OR BRAIN DEADENING?

Most of us spend between 11 and 17 years in full-time education. For some, learning goes on for the whole of his or her life. In fact, given the brain's immense capabilities, it is very sad when we don't continue to expand our knowledge and skills throughout our lifetime. However, it is easy to confuse learning and education. The formal education system has many worthy roles – but they aren't all about stretching the brain. In fact, while good education will improve your ability to gather and process knowledge, and will generally not influence your memory skills either way, there are few formal education systems that don't decrease an individual's creativity.

There are perfectly good reasons for this. At worst, creativity can be a survival issue. Trying out different ways to leave a skyscraper may be creative, but flinging yourself from a 20th floor window is not a life-enhancing move. Even when creativity is in theory safe, when dealing with the cushioned world of ideas, it can be threatening to education. Most educational regimes depend on getting through a set curriculum in a set time. Being too creative will disrupt this. A practical teacher is looking to get the answers that examiners want, not the most creative answer.

The result of this is that every individual suffers a reduction in creativity between starting school and leaving it. Worse still, peer pressure in schools often calls for conformity and hence more loss of creativity. If this sounds an indictment of schools, it isn't meant to be. Unless we wanted schools to do something completely different, some degree of conformity is essential. But this early training does mean that we have to go even further to give the brain a workout after school has finished with it.

KNOWLEDGE, MEMORY AND CREATIVITY

The brain has a vast array of functions and capabilities, but for the purposes of this book we are going to concentrate on three principal areas – knowledge, memory and creativity. Each represents a particular aspect of what would generally be regarded as brainpower. How effective you are at building your store of knowledge and making use of it, how good your memory is and how easily you can be creative all contribute to the overall capabilities of your brain. After using some of these exercises you will have the opportunity to develop all three.

CONSCIOUS AND UNCONSCIOUS ACTIVITY

As psychology professor Guy Claxton points out in *Hare Brain, Tortoise Mind* (see Chapter 6 for details), we are accustomed to give much weight to the conscious, step-by-step aspects of thought. Everything from scientific research to detective work places great emphasis on the objective, reasoned view (in fact, even Claxton's book is full of scientific, reasoned argument). Yet we know that the unconscious mind is capable of remarkable things. We have all experienced the sudden realisation that we have just undertaken a complex task like driving a car on automatic pilot. We have all been unable to remember something, no matter how hard we try, only to have the fact resurface soon after apparently ceasing to think about it.

A number of these exercises seek to push some more of your thinking into the unconscious – to make use of the benefits available if you are prepared to give pressurized reasoning a break and allow your whole brain to address a need. Such exercises can seem a little waffly. It's easy to think, 'what am I doing examining my navel, when I want to get on with something practical?'. The fact is that these are practical exercises, but because they take an unusual direction they may seem rather different.

It's not uncommon for proponents of delving into the unconscious to mention how much this follows a strong tradition of Eastern philosophy and mysticism. While this is true, it can be misleading. Although Western philosophy has often used a more deterministic approach, Western and Middle Eastern religions have just as strong a tradition of meditation and reflection as those of the Far East. There is no need whatsoever to stray into Zen or Buddhism if these conflict with your own beliefs – in fact, the Judeo-Christian-Moslem approach is more practical in that it combines both the conscious and unconscious modes, while Eastern practices tend to focus solely on the unconscious. If you have no religious beliefs at all, don't worry – the weight of scientific research supports the practical value of this approach, whatever the underlying regime.

USING THIS BOOK

Each exercise in *Instant Brainpower* is presented in a standard format with brief details of any preparation required, running time, resources used and the timescale of its application, followed by a description of the exercise itself. Next come suggestions for feedback, comments on the outcome and possible variations on the technique. The final part of the entry is the star rating. This is a quick reference to show how the particular exercise impacts on your knowledge, management skills, memory and creativity – and how much fun it is likely to be. As much as possible, to keep with the 'instant' theme, the exercises require minimal preparation, but some exercises requiring a little more work beforehand are included as they can sometimes be particularly effective. Note that timings are a minimum – you can take longer over most of the exercises if it is appropriate.

How you use the exercises very much depends on your approach to life. There is nothing wrong with working through the whole book in sequence – different types of exercise follow one another for this reason. Alternatively, the tables in the Appendix offer a number of ways of picking an exercise. There is a random selection table as a way of dipping into the exercises without getting into a rut. And there are tables arranging the exercises by how well they scored in the various star ratings. Use the exercises however they best fit with your schedule with the proviso that brain skills require regular practice, and that you shouldn't skip an exercise because it hasn't an immediate application – remember these are the equivalent of bodybuilding for the brain. You are not always looking for an immediate reaction, but for a broad improvement.

2

GETTING THE KNOWLEDGE

WHAT IS KNOWLEDGE?

Despite sounding like one of those deep questions asked of mystics living in caves at the top of mountains (who then reply, enigmatically, 'a fish'), this is both a serious and tricky question. Knowledge stands at the top of the pyramid that begins with data, builds through information and climaxes with knowledge itself.

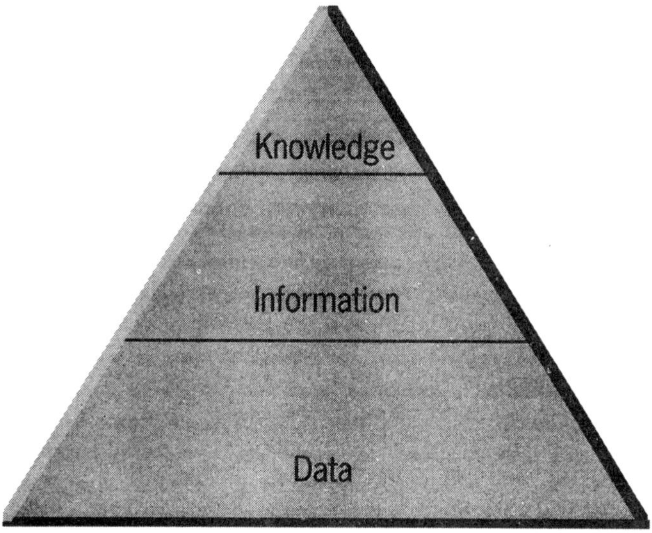

Data is a mass of facts without any interpretation. The results of a series of races, or football matches, for example, are data. Information is a combination of data and analysis. The data is taken and something is done with it. The result might be data presented in a certain way to pull out a trend, or might be a commentary saying why the data is how it is – this is information. Knowledge, though, is something more. Knowledge is the combination of data and information with the active elements of a person's brain that enable that person to turn data into information. Knowledge pulls together experience and reasoning to deal with a new circumstance. Knowledge is the currency of the expert.

In the 21st century world of frantic change and information overload, knowledge is the lifeline we all need. When things are consistent and calm, it's easy to manage with a set of rules. That's what most early 20th century management was about – rules – and management by rule has carried on mostly by inertia to the present day. Unfortunately rules break down when everything is in flux. You can't depend on them – you need to have a set of principles and the knowledge to apply them appropriately to the new situation. That's why experts are so valued now, and why the ability to handle knowledge has become one of the principal skills for the individual.

THE KNOWLEDGE MANAGEMENT BUSINESS

Recognising the importance of knowledge to business (and academia), a whole new discipline of knowledge management has congealed from a number of existing areas – taking bits of computer science, artificial intelligence, cognitive science, philosophy, and more. There are books and even magazines dedicated to supporting 'knowledge professionals'. I have one in front of me at the moment that boasts headlines like 'Xerox on harmonising and sharing' and 'Data mining in depth'.

Knowledge management is not a bad thing, but it can overemphasize the non-human aspects of knowledge. Knowledge management professionals sometimes act as if knowledge can be extracted out of people and put in a box, to be pulled out whenever it is needed. It isn't surprising that they sometimes give this impression, because it's what businesses want to hear. Experts are expensive, and have a tendency to either go over to the opposition or to die. If it were possible to extract their knowledge and put it in a 'knowledge base', you could dispose of the expert.

Forgetting for a moment the expert's feelings about this (and any expert worth the title is going to make sure that the system can't match his or her own skills), the whole concept is flawed. One of the significant differences between knowledge and information is that knowledge has a live component. A human component. Once it is extracted, the knowledge becomes dead, and the flexibility to apply it to different situations and to evolve it over time goes away. The knowledge loses its prime value.

This isn't to say that knowledge management is a bad thing, just that it should be seen as a complement to using human experts, not a replacement for them. Abstract knowledge management isn't the concern of this book. We are looking to build your human knowledge skills.

A LOT OF THEORY

One of the problems with knowledge management is pinning down just what it is. A broad picture starts with the skills required to gather data, whether from people (hence interviewing skills, producing appropriate questions, understanding conversation, etc), or from recorded sources. Next something has to be done with this data (actually a mix of data and information). This requires the ability to understand existing structures and to provide new structures where none exist, or more are needed. The knowledge manager needs to be able to represent that mass of data and information in a practical way.

Next, the knowledge manager needs to 'internalize' the knowledge, making use of a whole gamut of literacy skills from perception to language, pulling the structured information into his or her own model of the world. Finally, it may be appropriate to share that knowledge, whether through simple writing or using information technology to disseminate and store knowledge and information. (Bear in mind that knowledge isn't the same as information – to store knowledge in a computer implies some form of artificial intelligence.) All this falls under the knowledge management umbrella.

WHAT ABOUT THE INTERNET?

What indeed. In one sense there's nothing revolutionary about the Internet. It's just more of the same that we've always had to extend our personal knowledge library and network – communications and information retrieval. What is revolutionary is the scale and accessibility of the Internet. Here are near-instantaneous communications with other people from whom you may be able to extract knowledge and information. If you can find the information you want, here is a vast library to extend your personal information base, available at the desktop, 24 hours a day.

This book isn't the place to learn about using the Internet more effectively to expand your knowledge network. There are a couple of exercises touching on the Internet, but to find out more, see *Mining the Internet*, also from Kogan Page (more information on page 106).

BECOMING BETTER KNOWLEDGE MANAGERS

For the purposes of this book, we can be relatively simplistic and consider knowledge management to be the skills needed to find and process information, to categorize and structure it and to incorporate it into your personal knowledge base. This 'knowledge base' isn't some mighty computer program that knows everything, but the sum of what you hold in your memory, and what you know how to get hold of in your library. The library isn't just what is on your bookshelves, but CD-ROMs, information on paper and on your computer, information on the Internet and at your local library. What turns this from information into knowledge is its integration into your expertize – your ability to find, call on and integrate the right information at the right time to carry out your purposes. (And I said, it would be simplistic. If this sounded complicated, try reading a conventional book on knowledge management.)

3

MEMORY

HOW MEMORY WORKS

You have two forms of memory – short-term and long-term (technically there's a third, medium-term memory that sits in between, but let's not complicate matters). Short-term memory is a working store, like the memory of a computer, which is lost when the computer is turned off. Your short-term memory is very small – in essence you can only cope with a handful of items, typically around seven at a time, in short-term memory. When you plug something else into the memory, it pushes an item out. You can see short-term memory in action between looking up a phone number in a book and dialling it. It might seem strange, if short-term memory is limited to around seven items, that you can cope with a ten-digit number. Luckily, human memory is more flexible than a computer. Where everything in the computer's memory is made up of simple bits – 0 or 1 – human memory can hold an image or a word as a single item. Familiar dialling codes, for instance, are only a single item, leaving space (just about) for the rest of the number.

Long-term memory is a whole different ball game. To all intents and purposes the capacity is unlimited. You have plenty of storage for everything you are ever likely to remember. But getting something into long-term memory is not as simple as short-term memory. Using short-term memory is an act of will that is implemented immediately – getting something into long-term memory requires work.

This is where the lack of training in using your brain becomes a real disadvantage. Unless you understand how the brain works, the actions needed to lock something into memory seem bizarre. However, once you understand that you hold images in a sort of map of what you are remembering, it becomes more obvious. To fix something in your memory, it is best if you can see it in image form – hence the success of pictorial representations of information like mind maps – with the most vivid (in fact lurid) images you can imagine. To keep it there, you also need recaps. Ideally, these should come straight after taking in the material, a few hours later and a few days later, with a top-up after a month and six months.

FORGETTING

Once we've got something into long-term memory, it's a reasonable question to ask why we ever forget it. After all, it would be very useful to be able to recall anything you've previously committed to memory. Forgetting isn't a simple process. When you have 'forgotten' something, it hasn't necessarily left your memory entirely. What is more likely is that it is partially lost, or that the pathways to reach it are not well-trodden and have become overgrown. We've all forgotten something, only to have it pop up unexpectedly a few hours later. In such a circumstance it clearly wasn't erased from memory, but simply mislaid.

Although memories might sometimes go away because of the classic Freudian concept of repression (it was just too horrible to remember), generally it seems that we can't remember something either because we're in the wrong frame of mind to do so, or because other memories have confused and messed up the pathways to the particular thing you want to recall. It's not that you've run out of memory capacity – that isn't going to happen – but that the string of images and associations you use to recall a memory has become overlaid by other, similar images and associations. You might find it difficult to recall a beach holiday 10 years ago, because other beach holidays since then have got in the way.

If this is the principal reason for forgetting, we can easily combat it by a combination of recaps and ensuring that the associated imagery is as strong and individual as is possible.

MEMORY MAGIC

We've already established that the brain has a pretty amazing capacity – so how come you can never remember where you left your keys? Memory can both deliver amazing feats with startling regularity and let us down on apparent basics.

Many people have trouble remembering names, and applying them to people, but we are all superbly well equipped to remember faces. Most of us remember thousands, from friends and family to actors on TV and casual acquaintances at work. Yet try to describe someone you know well in a way that will distinguish them from everyone else in your gallery of faces and you will have real trouble. The basic features don't vary all that much. In remembering a face, we pull together a whole complex set of shapes, patterns and colours. In fact, remembering a person also includes lots of clues from the rest of their body and their movements, which is why it's harder to recognize a photograph than a real person. About a year ago, I was on a tube station in London, waiting for a train. I happened to glance into the office on the platform. I recognized one of the two men in the office. This was despite the fact that he had nothing to do with London Underground, so I wouldn't expect to see him there, and that the glass was darkened, and that he had his back to me. I recognized him entirely from the way he moved.

Another example of memory failing is with telephone numbers. They just aren't easy to remember. I once spent a whole evening in a hotel room trying to remember my own home number. For some reason it had slipped my mind, and the more I tried to summon it back, the more it evaded capture. If such a well-known number can slip from your memory, it's not surprising that other telephone numbers are hard to keep hold of. In part, it's because we aren't good at remembering more than six to eight items in a group and, despite the telephone companies attempts to group numbers accordingly, a telephone number is too long. But it's also because they are so impersonal and lacking in images. Unlike computer memory, human memory isn't about numbers or characters, it's about images. So despite the fuss TV presenters make about the complexity of e-mail addresses, it's an awful lot easier to remember the words (often with visual connotations) than it is to remember a telephone number.

So what do you do if you can't remember numbers or names? And how come some people who don't have eidetic memories (the rare capability to see a whole page of text and instantly commit it to memory) can do amazing feats like remembering the names of everyone in an audience or memorizing a phone book? Like most magic, it's a trick. At least since the ancient Greeks it has been known that you can use little tricks to fix information in memory. These mnemonics (that's the Greeks for you) generally work by linking the item to be remembered to an image to make the memory more capable of handling it. We'll see a number of practical applications of these tricks in the exercises.

What often comes hardest is accepting that these tricks work for everyone. Okay, the memory man on the TV can do it, but perhaps he is especially skilled. Not at all – everyone is capable of these tricks. As a trivial example, when I first came across such memory techniques (specifically *Name game*, 5.19), about 20 years ago, I went into a shop the same lunchtime and memorized the name of the first person I saw with a name badge. It was Mrs Anne Hibble. Without conscious effort, that once-sighted name has stayed with me for 20 years. There is a natural laziness that prevents people from using these techniques unless they are a regular habit. Like most skills, they need practising and keeping polished.

THE VALUE OF MEMORY

Before leaving memory, it's worth establishing that there is some point to it. First let's deal with the problem some people have with memory tricks. 'We don't want to do tricks', they say, 'we want to learn how to use proper memory better'. This is a misunderstanding. Mnemonics and the like are only tricks because they make something apparently difficult actually easy. What they are doing is converting the sort of item that your brain doesn't like handling into the sort of item it does. This is absolutely 'learning how to use proper memory better' – it just seems artificial.

But is there any reason for having a good memory these days, when everything can be calculated with ease, retrieved from a database or found on the Web? Absolutely. You have a huge wasted memory capacity that will serve you much more flexibly and quicker than resorting to a computer. By using a few memory tricks you can get huge personal advantage. For example, even if they know they are being manipulated, people react better if you call them by name – they just can't help it. If you can remember the names of everyone in a new team or group, you will be more effective at whatever it is you are trying to do with them. And in many other circumstances, memory can save you time and improve what you are trying to do. It's not a matter of being an information magpie and trying to remember everything about everything, but about capturing the information that will be of most value to you and having it readily to hand.

4

CREATIVITY

CREATIVITY CENTRAL

Creativity is the brain's ultimate weapon in an uncertain world. Without creativity we are restricted to reacting to set rules in dealing with life. Rules are fine at times of constancy. But there has never been a less constant time than the present. A few hundred years ago, you could pass through a whole century and not be aware of any significant change to the way things were. Looking back on the 20th century, there is hardly anything in our everyday experience that wasn't hugely changed from our predecessors. Change is here and change is accelerating. Instead of rules, we need the ability to be both proactive and to react flexibly and originally – all of which calls for creativity.

BORN WITH IT?

It is widely recognized that some people are more creative than others. Most of us are happy to bow to the creative genius of others, thinking that we're just down-to-earth people who might be reasonably good at picking up an idea and running with it, but we don't expect to be too creative. If your creativity were solely down to what you were born with, that would be the end of the story – but it's not that simple.

Just as channelling (as in education at school) that requires 'the right answer' to a question can reduce personal creativity, there are simple techniques and exercises that can increase personal creativity. This shouldn't be too surprising. In the end, creativity is all about being able to see outside the habitual tunnel of thought we all operate within. It shouldn't be too surprising that there are techniques that will move us out of the tunnel, opening up new prospects and possibilities. These techniques are not themselves creative, but act as a catalyst releasing the potential creativity in all of us.

OTHER APPROACHES

There are a number of ways of approaching the release of creativity. The companions to this book, *Instant Creativity* and *Instant Teamwork*, both address creativity. *Instant Creativity* provides a set of techniques that can be applied by individuals or teams to generate new ideas or to come up with potential solutions to a specific problem. These are mechanisms for propelling you out of the tunnel of habitual thought at a particular moment, for a particular purpose.

Instant Teamwork, on the other hand, provides more general exercises to get a team working more effectively and creatively together. Here the aim is break down the barriers to creativity that we naturally erect, particularly when with others who may ridicule our ideas.

This book, fitting with the brainpower topic, takes a third approach. It is aimed at individuals, but instead of providing a specific technique to propel you out of the tunnel, it aims to illuminate the tunnel, so that it becomes natural to walk straight through the transparent sides. Alongside the exercises to improve your knowledge management and memory are techniques to make it more natural to be creative without ever resorting to a technique.

THE CREATIVITY WORKOUT

The ability to expand our creative capabilities is obviously highly desirable, but how is it to be achieved? Unlike creativity techniques, which are mechanistic processes that can reliably push an individual in a new direction, a general increase in the level of creativity is a much broader aim.

Much of the creativity workout consists of exercises for your personal creativity. It might be true that school shuts down much of our creativity, but at least it gave us some opportunity for practice. For many of us, the day we left school is the last time we attempted creative writing or art. For some people, it's even the last time we read any fiction. That has to stop. If you want to enhance your personal creativity, you need to get some practice at these creative forms.

Note that this isn't an end in itself. It doesn't matter if you produce a story or picture then throw it away (once you've learnt something). The aim is not to turn you into a creative writer or an artist, but to increase the ease with which you take that creative step out of the tunnel – to make it just as natural as operating a spreadsheet or driving a car. If you have young children, you have a natural opportunity to expand your creativity workout. Young children are always asking you to draw something or to tell them a story. Your natural inclination may be to say, 'I can't draw' or, 'I'll read you a story' – but take the opportunity that is being offered you to stretch your own creativity with a low-risk audience.

Apart from the traditional creative elements, we will also be stretching our creative muscles using puzzles and by stimulating different types of thinking. Don't be put off if either of these doesn't come naturally to you. You don't have to actually enjoy puzzles (I don't) to get the benefit, any more than you need to enjoy running to get fit that way – although obviously it doesn't do any harm if you do enjoy them. Similarly, you may be sceptical of the value of techniques that explore your ways of thinking – perhaps it seems to be getting too close to the whole alternative therapy, touchy-feely business for you. Bear in mind that fuzzy alternative lifestyles and Eastern philosophies are not the basis for such exercises, but concrete research into the way the mind works.

5

THE EXERCISES

5.1 On the box

Preparation Check TV schedules.
Running time 30 minutes.
Resources TV; notepad.
Frequency Once.

Look through the TV schedules and find a number of different types of programme where interviewing (in the broadest sense) is liable to take place. Watch several separate chunks of interviewing in action – perhaps five minutes at a time. Concentrate on what the interviewer is doing. Make notes of how he or she tries to extract information from the interviewee. Look for open or closed questions (can they be answered with a single word, or do they require detailed description). Look for questions that elicit facts, and questions that elicit feelings. How does the interviewer handle an interviewee who is trying to avoid the question?

Feedback Try to distil down the most effective aspects of the interviewer's technique as a set of personal pointers. Even if your role doesn't involve explicit interviewing, these techniques will be useful. Whenever you are talking to someone else to increase your knowledge level you are, in fact, interviewing. Most of us could improve our skills here significantly. A key aspect of doing this well, which the professionals on TV have off to a fine art, is to minimize the obtrusiveness of the techniques they are using. It is the answers people are interested in, rather than the questions. Because of this, you will have to concentrate with unusual care on just what the interviewer is doing.

Outcome By incorporating a few of the tricks of professional interviewers into your repertoire you can increase the effectiveness of your knowledge gathering significantly.

Variations If you get the chance, also try this out with speech radio, particularly in a heavyweight political or news show. Consider taping the interviews (speech or TV) so you can play them back a few times to pick up the fine detail.

Knowledge	✪✪✪✪
Memory	✪
Creativity	✪
Fun	✪✪

5.2 Water into wine

Preparation None.
Running time Five minutes.
Resources None.
Frequency Once.

I have two bottles, one containing water and the other containing wine. I pour one measure of wine into the water bottle. I then pour an equal measure from the water bottle back into the wine bottle. At the end, there is just as much water in the wine as there is wine in the water. Which of the following have to be true to make this possible (you can choose more than one):

- The bottles are the same size.
- The water and wine are thoroughly mixed after the measure is poured into the water bottle.
- The wine and water have to be thoroughly mixed after the measure is poured back into the wine bottle.
- The wine has the same density as the water.
- The water and wine are miscible.

...or is it impossible to be certain that there is just as much water in the wine as there is wine in the water?

Feedback Don't go any further until you've attempted some sort of answer. Last chance to consider your answer. In fact, none of the conditions have to hold true – there will always be just as much wine in the water as water in the wine. Think of it like this: at the end of the process, the wine bottle holds exactly the same amount as it did initially, so it must have had exactly the same amount of water added to it as wine was removed.

Outcome Notice how the way that the question was phrased can distract you from the true facts. Even if you got the right answer, the chances are that the phrasing proved a distraction. You probably worried about partial mixing of water and wine, for example. Sometimes rephrasing the question is an essential for knowledge gathering and creativity.

Variations Look at a few real-life problems you've dealt with and think how much you have assumed about the question that had to be answered.

Knowledge	✪✪✪✪
Memory	✪
Creativity	✪✪✪✪
Fun	✪✪✪

5.3 Broken record

Preparation Invent scenario.
Running time Five minutes.
Resources A stooge.
Frequency Once.

Imagine a situation in which you have to complain about something. Persuade a colleague to act as a stooge in trying out this scenario. His or her role is to counter your request. For example, you could be taking back a broken product and demanding a replacement, or asking for a refund in a restaurant. Use the traditional assertion technique of 'broken record'. Simply repeat your request whatever the stooge says. Don't go on too long, but do go on significantly longer than the comfort factor will allow.

Feedback Sometimes when you are trying to gain knowledge you will be resisted. This could be for three reasons – because the person doesn't know, because he or she simply doesn't want to tell you, or because he or she doesn't understand your question. This exercise gives some practice in dealing with the second possibility. Make sure that you keep your repeated request for the information low key and friendly. Nod, agree, say, 'Yes, I see' to the other person's reasons for not coming up with the goods – then ask again. This technique is best used face to face; it is too easy for the other person to just put the phone down. If you find it very difficult, practise some more – it becomes relatively easy and can even be enjoyable.

Outcome It is surprising how often this technique will whittle away resistance and get a result. It's not one you want to use too often, or somewhere you are a regular visitor, but it can sometimes be very effective.

Variations If there is a genuine circumstance when you can practise the technique, so much the better. This could either be in the sort of scenario used here (complaint) or when you are trying to get information from a reluctant source.

Knowledge	✪✪✪✪
Memory	✪
Creativity	✪
Fun	✪✪

5.4 Category magic

Preparation A set of information you need to structure or understand.
Running time 10 minutes.
Resources Notepad.
Frequency Once.

Although the brain probably doesn't use categories to store information, it's a good way to break down concepts and facts to make them easier to understand. Sometimes categories are obvious. They may be 'good' or 'bad', or simple context categories like 'make of car' or 'type of Web site'. In other cases, the categories don't spring to mind. This technique will help in such circumstances.

Spend a minute or two jotting down bullet points from the information. Note key aspects of the information, specific items of information that can stand alone. Now take three of these items at random. You could use a spreadsheet or write your items on cards to do this. See if you can find a feature that two items share, but the third doesn't. Note down this feature as a category.

Select three at random again and repeat the process several times. There is no right or wrong number – do it until you seem to be running out of new categories or you've got at least 10 categories.

Look through the categories list, seeing if any sensibly combine. Then try to allocate the items of information to the different categories. You may need to revisit category generation if you don't have a good set, but it's surprising how often you will have.

Feedback This approach won't generate every possible category – but you are just trying to find a structure that works. If you are comfortable with the outcome, the categories are fine.

Outcome With a little practice, the categories often come together without needing this technique, but it's valuable if you have trouble generating categories. It can be used for everything from structuring information to generating an outline report.

Variations If you don't have a set of information you need to structure right now, spend a minute writing down at least 10 reasons why you like your favourite thing, and use those instead to get the practice.

Knowledge	✪✪✪✪
Memory	✪✪✪
Creativity	✪
Fun	✪

5.5 Doing and knowing

Preparation None.
Running time Five minutes.
Resources Notepad.
Frequency Once.

Think back over the last week and pick out between half a dozen and 10 activities you undertook. Make them quite different – anything from reading a newspaper to performing brain surgery. List the activities, and rate each out of 10 for your doing ability – your skill level, and your knowing ability – your knowledge level.

Next, note activities where there is a significant difference between the two scores. What does this imply to you about the activity and your approach to it? Remember, in this context, 'knowing' is about the activity itself, so in our example of reading a newspaper, it would involve your knowledge of the mechanics of reading, not your familiarity with current affairs.

Finally, where you have high knowledge scores, think how you might be able to use that knowledge in totally different circumstances. Where you have low scores, think how you might be able to apply some other source of knowledge if you had need of it. What if you had to explain one of these topics to a group of children, or needed to find a viable alternative – what knowledge would you call upon?

Feedback Often we have to transfer knowledge from one area to another, or combine bits of knowledge to make a new whole. It is interesting to see how much our own knowledge correlates with our skills. It is quite possible, for instance to be a great computer programmer without having the faintest idea how computers work, or to be an excellent woodcarver with no knowledge of the chemical makeup of wood.

Outcome The aim of this exercise is to improve your understanding of what knowledge is, and to be more aware of how you deal with gaps in your knowledge, an essential process in good knowledge management.

Variations Think about valuations. Do we think more of highly skilled people in a particular field or of highly knowledgeable people? Do these valuations vary from field to field?

Knowledge	✪✪✪✪
Memory	✪
Creativity	✪
Fun	✪✪

5.6 Metaphorically speaking

Preparation None.
Running time Five minutes.
Resources Newspaper or Web news site; notepad.
Frequency Several times.

Use a newspaper (or a Web news site) to generate a list of five items. They could be people, places, events, objects – anything, as long as the five are quite different. Now spend no more than a minute on each item, jotting down a series of metaphors with short reasons attached. For example, one of the items in today's news is about London's Docklands. I might think Docklands is like:

- A forest – because there are lots of tall buildings.
- A graveyard – all the monuments.
- A beehive – activity in an alien environment.
- etc.

Feedback Don't think too much about your metaphors, just let them flow. If you have real problems getting started, think of the key attributes of whatever you are trying to create a metaphor for, then think of other things with similar attributes. But you should aim to make metaphor formation natural, as it will produce attributes you weren't consciously aware of. Getting better at metaphor formation supports all three of the *Instant Brainpower* skill areas. Knowledge and memory both depend on metaphor and imagery, to cope with new but similar cases and to store information in the image-oriented brain. Metaphor is also a valuable way of improving personal creativity. A metaphor can often be used to solve a problem or to generate an idea. By saying that a problem is like something, we can find new approaches. Finally, metaphor is valuable in improving your personal creativity when writing – it's powerful stuff.

Outcome Metaphor is a cornerstone of brain skills; this exercise enhances your brain's ability to deal with difficult problems and to remember important issues.

Variations Five minutes is enough for one session, but this is an exercise you could repeat regularly for a while. Perhaps weekly for a month, then reinforce every few months, keeping the metaphorical (in more than one sense) mental muscles in trim.

Knowledge	✪✪✪✪
Memory	✪✪✪
Creativity	✪✪✪✪
Fun	✪✪✪

5.7 Sense and sensibility

Preparation None.
Running time 10 minutes.
Resources Magazine; notepad.
Frequency Once.

How we handle information and transform it into knowledge is very much influenced by our senses. Experts in the knowledge management field, never willing to use a simple word where a complex one will do, refer to these sensory views of the world as modalities.

Get hold of a magazine with reasonably long features (or take one of your own pieces of prose if you regularly write articles). Look through one article. Don't worry about the content of the piece – instead note how it makes use of the modalities: sight, hearing, touch (and motion), taste and smell. See if the writer has a particular bias. Does this give the piece a specific flavour? Could it have an effect on how you react to the article?

Feedback It's very difficult to deal with the world without using modalities. Notice how in the previous section, modalities were described as 'sensory views of the world'. The use of the term 'view' is itself a modality. No one actually viewed anything. Similarly, the term 'flavour' was used later on without anything being tasted. You may have to read the article a couple of times, as it is very easy to skip over modalities – they are such a natural part of the language, and often appear as stock phrases (like 'that rings a bell' or 'this needs hands-on management').

Outcome The main aim here is to understand how these sensory terms are used to fit information into our understanding. If you can be more aware of the process that is underway you can help to improve your own knowledge management.

Variations With a little more time, even if you haven't got a piece of your own prose, write a page or two describing one of your more complex pieces of knowledge in a way that a lay person could understand it. See how you make use of this sensory imagery.

Knowledge	✪✪✪✪
Memory	✪✪
Creativity	✪
Fun	✪✪

5.8 Altered states

Preparation None.
Running time 10 minutes.
Resources None.
Frequency Oncc.

Sit in a comfortable chair. Close your eyes. Think of an occasion when you were engaged in a very successful activity, where everything went well, when you felt confident, relaxed and in control. As much as possible, imagine yourself into that memory. Take in as much as you can of your situation, any sights and sounds, smells and touches you experienced.

When you are comfortably feeling part of the memory, choose a particular combination of senses and feelings which can act as a key to trigger the memory in as much detail as possible. If there was just one thing that could get you back to this memory as quickly as possible, what would it be?

Now get out of the chair, move around a little, then try the key to bring back the memory.

Feedback This technique is based on the approach that psychologist Mihaly Csikszentmihalyi calls 'flow'. This is an approach that has been adopted by a number of successful athletes who need to maximize their performance at a particular time. The aspect we are dealing with is the way that recalling as completely as possible a previous state of mind will move your current state into a similar position. This is manipulating the brain at the most basic level.

Outcome By using the key memory to recall a state of mind where you were confident, in control and successful, you can bring yourself into a similar state in the present. The simple presence of such confidence gives you a better chance of success in an activity.

Variations When you have done the basic exercise, try using the key to bring back the memory in positions of greater and greater stress. To begin with it will be difficult to manage quickly enough and in the face of distraction, but you should be able to do it almost instantly with practice.

Knowledge	✪✪✪
Memory	✪✪✪
Creativity	✪✪✪
Fun	✪✪

5.9 All that glisters

Preparation None.
Running time Five minutes.
Resources Notepad.
Frequency Once.

Spend a minute jotting down all the regular sources of information you access to keep up to date in your areas of expertise. Include all sorts of media – magazines and journals, TV, radio, newspapers, the Internet, etc. Against each source, estimate how much time a week you spend with it.

Do you feel you are totally on top of your subject(s), or are there not enough hours in the day to keep up to date? If you feel you are being left behind, try this approach. Select a subset of your regular sources that you feel will give a good background. Instead of trying to absorb everything, limit yourself to this background information, but know how to pull in extra information at a moment's notice. See *Mining the Internet* in Chapter 6 for one way of doing this.

Feedback There has never been such an age of information overload. It's hard enough keeping up with your specialities without having to chase down all the general information needed to make you a well-rounded person. An essential for managing your own state of knowledge is being aware that it is impossible to take in everything. There comes a point where being an information magpie and trying to pick up every little snippet on every possibly relevant topic simply gets in the way. There are some special cases here – it probably is a good thing to be a magpie when it comes to your contacts (see *The little black book*, 5.26), but not when you are trying to absorb information.

Outcome By understanding that you can't possibly take in everything, finding routes to get enough general background and establishing the ability to pull in detailed information as and when required without storing it up, you can stay on top of information overload.

Variations Consider different ways of getting your information, both background and in-depth. Perhaps there are industry summaries or news summaries that will give you the basics without needing to search through many sources.

Knowledge	✪✪✪✪
Memory	✪✪
Creativity	✪
Fun	✪✪

5.10 Chunks and breaks

Preparation None.
Running time Five minutes.
Resources Notepad.
Frequency Once.

We've all been in the situation. You have to give a presentation/write an article/take an exam. Time is short and there is a huge amount of information that you need to digest and turn into knowledge. So you read long into the night, steaming open your eyelids with cups of coffee, hardly stopping at all.

Unfortunately there is overwhelming evidence that this is not a great way to absorb information. The amount you retain drops off after time, but breaking the session into chunks with a series of short breaks, means more can be absorbed. There isn't a magic length for the chunks – experimenting may help – but it is usually between 15 minutes and an hour, with breaks of around five minutes to overcome the deterioration in retention.

In the few minutes allowed for this exercise, you aren't going to actually work through some information. Instead, take a task you have ahead (or invent one for the exercise), and rough out a schedule of chunks and breaks. Next time you actually do this kind of work, make sure you use your schedule.

Feedback It's tempting to carry on if everything is going excellently. This may be valid for pure productive work, but doesn't apply where your aim is to learn and absorb. However well it seems things are going, your ability to remember will benefit from breaks. The break should be something completely different, involving a different use of the mind. Getting out in the fresh air for a few minutes and unwinding is ideal.

Outcome Breaking things into chunks makes a lot of sense, but it's human nature to forge on and try to get through, especially under pressure. It often takes tight scheduling to get yourself breaking to begin with – but persevere for improved retention and enhanced knowledge.

Variations Try different chunkings to see which works best for you. The natural tendency is to try for the longest chunks as these seem more efficient. It isn't necessarily the case.

Knowledge	✪✪✪
Memory	✪✪✪✪
Creativity	✪✪
Fun	✪✪

5.11 Extremes

Preparation None.
Running time Five minutes.
Resources Quiet environment.
Frequency Once.

A lot of memory techniques use imagery. Whether you want to remember a set of numbers, people's names or the contents of a textbook, imagery can help to fix the information in your mind. It is also an essential precursor to turning information into knowledge.

Let's say you had to remember the number 329. Using the rhyme method (see 5.22), you could portray this number as tree, shoe, line. A first try at an image might be a tree with a line of shoes leading away from it. The trouble is, this image is too mundane. The more dramatic, colourful (and yes, rude) the image is, the better it will stick. It would be better, for instance to imagine a huge, bright red, ravenous tree rampaging through a shopping mall, ripping people's shoes off (with the feet still inside them) and lining them up down the middle of the mall. A bit unpleasant and lurid? Exactly, that's the point.

Try it yourself on these two image chains. Don't worry about the techniques, just assume you have to strengthen up these chains of images. Dog, hole, telephone, tomato. Pizza, sumo wrestler, umbrella, elephant.

Feedback For some reason, even when an image is confined to your mind you can be just as squeamish, prudish and reasonable as you would be when chatting to the vicar. Let rip – be dramatic, be funny, be gross – it doesn't matter as long as the image is memorable and unique.

Outcome This exercise isn't a specific memory technique. Instead it supports all the others. By improving the vividness of your images, you will get better retention in the other techniques.

Variations This exercise uses the chains of images that are commonly generated by memory techniques. Try a similar approach with a simple story – if you can't be bothered to construct a story, take the basics of a well-known fairy tale, then push it to extremes.

Knowledge	✪✪✪
Memory	✪✪✪✪
Creativity	✪✪✪
Fun	✪✪✪

5.12 Surveying your mind

Preparation None.
Running time 10 minutes.
Resources Paper; flipchart or whiteboard and pens.
Frequency Regularly.

This technique is probably the best way to make notes or summarize content so that the brain can absorb it. There are many related techniques, generically called cognitive mapping. The best known variant, mind mapping, was developed by Tony Buzan, and is simple in concept. Start at the centre of a page or whiteboard and draw an image that represents the core of the issue. From this, radiate out branches that represent the major themes of the issue. From each of these, draw progressively lower and lower level themes.

On each branch write one or two keywords above the line to say what that issue is. For instance, one branch might be profit, splitting into costs and revenues, with revenues splitting into direct sales and indirect, while costs splits into the major cost drivers.

Try to make the image organic. Start with larger, fatter branches at the centre moving to smaller ones and eventually twigs at the extremities. You might also use different colours for each major branch (with subsidiaries the same colour as the major branch).

Feedback Don't get hung up on the process of drawing the map. The objective is an image-based overview of the information, not a work of art. It's important you stick to keywords, which retain the maximum amount of information with the minimum number of words.

Outcome This technique is a must if you really want to make the most of your brain. Conventional note taking can't compete for flexibility or retentiveness.

Variations There are many different ways to draw mind maps. *Mapping for memory*, 5.41, explores the use of colour and image to use a diagram to boost memory. For more information, see Tony and Barry Buzan's *The Mind Map Book* (details in Chapter 6). For simple note taking you can limit yourself to keywords and very simple images.

Knowledge	✪✪✪
Memory	✪✪✪✪
Creativity	✪✪✪
Fun	✪✪

5.13 Story chains

Preparation None.
Running time Five minutes.
Resources None.
Frequency Several times.

Quite often we need to remember a sequence of things, perhaps a procedure or a list. A story chain is the ideal mechanism. Build up a story involving the items in sequence. Use intense images. As you add each item, go back to the start of the story and briefly recap. So, for example, if I wanted to remember a telephone, a book and a car, I might have a story that was something like:

A huge purple telephone with thousands of legs was wandering through the woods when it tripped over a copy of the Yellow Pages. Unfortunately a fast Jaguar XK8 (British Racing Green) was hurtling past and squashed the telephone millipede flat.

Make it as lurid and personal as you can (I chose the Jaguar because I particularly like it). When you recap the story, don't run through a set of words, see it happening like a film unreeling in your mind.

Feedback You will find that you can hold a long list this way with very little effort. I've used it in one of those games where you go round saying, 'I've got a bag and in it is…' and everyone adds a new item. While the other players were floundering, I had no problem remembering 30 items. Because of the chain, it's slow for random access – to get to the 20th item you need to start at the beginning – but it still very useful. If you need some practice at constructing stories, see *Scribbling, 5.62.*

Outcome You will soon be effortlessly remembering long lists. It's easy to think that it's too much trouble to use a technique – so next time you have to order a round of drinks, try it.

Variations I've suggested recapping the list each time you add an item. With practice you can get away with an occasional recap. If you need to keep the list longer than a few hours, recap after a few hours, a couple of days and a week. Try it on different practical applications.

Knowledge	✪✪
Memory	✪✪✪✪
Creativity	✪
Fun	✪✪✪

5.14 Muddled model

Preparation None.
Running time Five minutes.
Resources None.
Frequency Once.

We understand the world by using models – it's impossible to grasp the whole, so we think of something simpler to get the picture. Sometimes we don't even know that our models are inaccurate or just plain wrong. For hundreds of years the model of the world as a flat disc was accepted. Even now, many people don't realize that the model of the atom as a set of electrons rotating round like planets round a central nucleus is a convenient fiction.

Sometimes inaccurate models are more appealing than the truth. An old legend says that the tide is caused by an immense crab coming out of its hole to hunt for food. The water rushes into the hole, causing the tide. This is both wrong and illogical, but who cares? It's a lovely picture. Take a pair of complex natural phenomena, like a rainbow or why the sky is blue. It doesn't matter whether or not you know the real reason, but for each phenomenon invent three totally different and probably incorrect models of what's happening. Go for appeal, not likeliness.

Feedback It sometimes takes a while to realize that most of what we 'know' is based on models, but then, unless the entire workings are visible and comprehensible, what else can we base our understanding on?

Outcome Incorrect models are a great source of creativity. Much fiction depends on the premise 'what if' – if an accepted model wasn't true. Science fiction does this boldly – what if people lived on a totally different planet, what if the French revolution had never happened. Conventional fiction has more subtle what ifs – what if a person behaved this way, or a relationship developed like this – but it is still modelling.

Variations This exercise increases your general creativity, but you could also apply the approach to a specific problem. Dream up totally fictional reasons why the problem could be occurring and solve them – then see what the solutions would do in the real world.

Knowledge	✪
Memory	✪
Creativity	✪✪✪✪
Fun	✪✪

5.15 One more time

Preparation Some learning required.
Running time Five minutes.
Resources Diary.
Frequency Regularly.

This is an exercise to undertake next time you have to learn something, whether it's a new system, first aid, your lines in a play or the contents of a business book. When you have undertaken a period of study (it sounds formal, but it might just be reading a few chapters of a book), plan out a review schedule. A good sequence to push information permanently into memory is to review after a few minutes, a day, a week, a month and six months. Don't leave it to chance. Slot something in your diary. We aren't talking a big commitment here – a review of an hour or two's work need only take a few minutes.

When you have got the schedule established, carry out the initial review. That's the end of the exercise right now, but remember to follow through.

Feedback This sort of reviewing is essential if you want a memory to become permanent. Even if you were learning something every day, the cumulative review time is not huge. The best way to minimize reviewing time while capturing most of the information is to use a mind map for review. See *Surveying your mind*, 5.12, for more details.

Outcome It might seem tediously mechanistic, but a schedule of review will ensure effective learning.

Variations You might successfully vary the frequency a little to taste, but the periods shown here usually provide the best retention.

Knowledge	✪✪✪
Memory	✪✪✪✪
Creativity	✪
Fun	✪

5.16 Take a note

Preparation Find a short piece of classical music.
Running time Five minutes.
Resources Notepad.
Frequency Once.

Find a short piece of classical music – around the five minute mark. It should be unfamiliar. Ask your friends and colleagues if you can borrow a CD or two. Find somewhere you can be undisturbed for five minutes. Sit comfortably with a notepad and listen to the music.

As you listen, let the music conjure up images. They can be obvious and direct (such as medieval church music evoking the image of a monastery) or quite unconnected with the original concept (a good example would be the way a Strauss waltz was used to accompany the shots of the rotating space station in the film 2001). Try to bring these images into as a solid perspective as possible.

As you get the images, jot down keyword notes on the pad. It's not essential, but it would help if you are familiar with mind mapping (see *Surveying your mind*, 5.12) before doing this. Don't aim for a detailed text description as this will get in the way of the visualisation – just try to capture the essence of what you see in your mind's eye.

Feedback Cast off any concerns that this is reminiscent of the sort of music appreciation you used to do at junior school. Your aim is much more concrete, and totally grown up. This is an exercise to give muscle tone to your knowledge building and creative skills.

Outcome This is a compound exercise, giving practice at forming clear images and processing fast incoming data and working under pressure. Every area of your brain skills will benefit from this practice.

Variations If you have difficulty forming images, try imagining you are watching a movie with this as the background music. What sort of thing might be happening on the screen? Don't stick to a single scene, but imagine the action changes with the music.

Knowledge	✪✪✪
Memory	✪✪✪
Creativity	✪✪✪✪
Fun	✪✪

5.17 Words of wisdom

Preparation None.
Running time Five minutes.
Resources Good dictionary; notepad.
Frequency Regularly.

Get hold of a good dictionary – not a concise volume, but one of the more detailed ones. Open the book at random three times, each time scanning until you reach an interesting word that you are vaguely familiar with but don't know how to use.

Make a few notes about each word. Use any imagery that springs to mind to fix it in your memory. Try to find an opportunity to use your three new words in the next few days.

Feedback There is a stock comedy character, not dissimilar to the train spotter, who is always fascinated by trivia and coming up with the obscure new words to irritate everyone. That isn't the intention. Don't force your words on people, only use them in an appropriate context. If there isn't one, don't worry too much.

Outcome This is a gradual, subtle exercise. Developing your ability to use language will make it easier to handle information. It also gives you a wider scope for creativity.

Variations Initially it's best to stick to words that you are vaguely familiar with but wouldn't use because you don't know them well enough. Even worse, you may find words that you do use, but without understanding their meaning. After a while, feel free to use more obscure words, but bear in mind that the purpose of language is to communicate: use less common words because they can put across a concept better, not to show how clever you are.

Knowledge	✪✪✪✪
Memory	✪
Creativity	✪✪✪
Fun	✪✪

5.18 Round the world

Preparation None.
Running time Five minutes.
Resources None.
Frequency Once.

This is an exercise in creative thinking. Don't skip it even if you don't like puzzles and logic problems. Exercise isn't always pleasant – it's the end result we are after, not the pleasure of getting there.

Imagine you had a very long rope with no stretch in it. This rope is just the right length to go round the equator of the world. Now imagine we added 3 metres to the length of the rope, and managed to lift it evenly off the surface of the planet to take up the slack. Guess what size of gap would be formed between the rope and the surface of the earth. Don't try to work it out, just guess. Then take an extra couple of minutes to think about how you would work out exactly how far the rope would be from the earth.

Feedback If you haven't already done the two parts of the problem above, do them now. Don't read any further. Last chance to consider your answer. The guess is usually that the rope lifts a tiny distance off the surface – perhaps a millimetre or less – because those three metres have to be evenly spread around about 40,000 kilometres of circumference. Unfortunately, circles don't work like that. The circumference is always $2\pi r$ – roughly six times the radius. So the radius was roughly C/6 where C is the circumference. Now the radius becomes (C+3)/6 – or C/6 +3/6 – in other words, the radius has increased by roughly 3/6, about half a metre. Much bigger than you might expect.

Outcome Our instinctive reaction to a problem is based on feel. Sometimes this is very valuable. Complex or fuzzy problems are often not amenable to detailed analysis. However, it is important to be aware that common sense can lead you astray: be prepared to challenge it.

Variations Look out for other opportunities to test and understand your intuition.

Knowledge	✪✪
Memory	✪
Creativity	✪✪✪✪
Fun	✪✪✪

5.19 Name game

Preparation Opportunity to meet people.
Running time Five minutes.
Resources None.
Frequency Once.

The number one memory problem is names. Few of us haven't at some point forgotten a name within 10 minutes of meeting someone. Yet we are all capable of remembering the names of a whole roomful of people without significant effort.

Next time you get a chance to meet new people, try this approach to remembering names. When you are introduced, repeat the name to yourself a couple of times. It can be subvocally, as long as it is not just a thought. As you do so, look for aspects of the name that you can pin an image on. Does it make you think of something? Does it sound like something or rhyme with something? Can you break it down into chunks which you can give a picture to? It's easier to do this with a name and a surname – if you are just introduced by first name, repeat their first name back to them with a questioning intonation to try to get the rest. Finally, imagine that person as part of the image. Make the whole thing as colourful, dramatic, sexy and ludicrous as possible.

Feedback Reinforce the image a few times as you spot the person again, making it come alive in your mind. This seems a lengthy process, but with practice, you can do it with a group of people as they go around the room saying who they are and what they do – a common practice at business meetings.

Outcome If you can be bothered to do this you will gain the huge advantage of being able to call someone by name, which will generally guarantee a better response from them.

Variations As practice helps, you could also try the technique before you get on to real people by looking for names of people you don't recognize in a newspaper. It won't be as effective as with real people, but it will give you some practice at the technique.

Knowledge	✪
Memory	✪✪✪✪
Creativity	✪
Fun	✪✪

5.20 Holistic awareness

Preparation None.
Running time 10 minutes.
Resources Quiet, comfortable location.
Frequency Once.

Don't panic if this sounds too 'knit your own yoghurt' – suspend your disbelief and try it before judging. It's difficult to phrase an exercise like this without occasionally using waffly terms, but the aim is not at all vague.

Find somewhere you can sit or lie comfortably without outside interference. Breathe slowly and regularly. Close your eyes (as long as you can do this without falling asleep). Visualize your body. Start at your head – think inside your head, then let your imagination work outwards, as if you were moving slowly outwards. Pause at the skin, thinking about the interface between your body and the world. Then work gradually down your body to your feet. Finally expand outwards, taking in all of the room.

Feedback It is important not to get analytical during this exercise. Your aim is not to think about what you visualize, merely to visualize it. Experience it with your virtual senses, but don't judge it or try to put what you experience into some sort of pigeonhole. Looking at yourself and your surroundings with such detachment can be very difficult to start with. You may need a few attempts to pull it off.

Outcome This exercise brings out two things – a feeling for abstract visualisation, and practice at focusing on a very specific subject in an overall way, rather than trying to break it down into detail or fit it into categories. This is a valuable underlying skill for dealing with knowledge, and can also help to improve your recall from memory.

Variations An extension to the exercise if you've time (or try it on a repeat session) is to continue after taking in the room. Return your awareness to your body. Start very gently to move one limb, then another. Try to keep your awareness working in the same holistic way as the motion occurs, experiencing the movement and the interface between your body and the world. *Strengthening your ghosts*, 5.67, carries on from here, helping to improve your mental imagery.

Knowledge	✪✪✪✪
Memory	✪✪✪
Creativity	✪✪
Fun	✪✪

5.21 Pub quiz

Preparation None.
Running time Five minutes.
Resources None.
Frequency Once.

This is a problem to give your brain skills a workout. Unlike some of the problems in this book it is amenable to logic – but the solution isn't particularly obvious.

Every day I go down to the local tube station and stand between eastbound and westbound platforms. Both eastbound and westbound trains come every 10 minutes. I catch whichever train comes first, travel one stop and get off. Then I go to the nearest pub for lunch. Somehow, though, I almost always go to The Grapes (the pub near the westbound station) rather than The Queen's Head (the pub near the eastbound station). In fact, I've noticed that, on average, I only go the Queen's Head once a fortnight. Why?

Feedback If you haven't already got an answer, try to jot one down now. Don't read any further. Last chance to consider your answer. Both eastbound and westbound trains run every 10 minutes. As it happens, the westbound trains arrive at the station one minute before the eastbound trains. Because of this, there is only one minute out of every 10 when the next train is the eastbound one. So I catch the eastbound train, on average, once every 10 tries, or once every two working weeks.

Outcome Unlike *Car and goats*, 5.33, this is a problem that is totally obvious once it is explained. Much creativity and knowledge is like this. The exercise is a valuable lesson in the mechanics of knowledge building, and in the requirement to explore the problem area before plunging in with a solution.

Variations Look for simple solutions to problems as well as the complex.

Knowledge	✪✪✪
Memory	✪
Creativity	✪✪✪
Fun	✪✪✪

5.22 Number rhymes

Preparation None.
Running time 10 minutes.
Resources Notepad.
Frequency Three times.

This is the classic method for remembering numbers. Each number is associated with a rhyming word. You can change the words if you can think of something better:

- 1 – gun
- 2 – shoe
- 3 – tree
- 4 – door
- 5 – hive
- 6 – sticks
- 7 – heaven
- 8 – weight
- 9 – line
- 10 (hence 0) – hen

The use is simple, but takes some practice. When you want to remember a number, make up a short story in your mind linking the nature of the number (eg, the person whose phone number it is) with the objects in the number rhyme in the right order. Make the story as vivid and pictorial as you can. Go through the story a number of times to reinforce it.

Feedback Before you do some actual stories, try drawing the items on a pad with the number to reinforce the rhyme. Try it out on some actual numbers you need to remember, but haven't yet had a chance to. Remember to make the little stories as extreme, colourful, dramatic or as rude as you can to fix the memory.

Outcome This may seem a trivial technique, but it will lock practically any number into your memory. To begin with you will use the story to recall it – later on the story will disappear, but the memory chain will remain.

Variations Although one try may be enough to convince you, it is best to try this out three times. Make the second time later the same day as the first. On that second attempt, do some new numbers, but also rerun the stories on the first set. Make the third try a few days later. Again, reinforce the earlier numbers. You might need to reinforce memories this way to make sure they stick. An alternative approach is found in *Number shapes*, 5.51 – you may find one approach suits you better.

Knowledge	✪✪
Memory	✪✪✪✪
Creativity	✪✪
Fun	✪✪✪

5.23 No time to read

Preparation None.
Running time 5 minutes.
Resources Diary.
Frequency Once.

Are you one of these people who has 'no time to read'? Whether or not this is the case, try out this exercise. Spend a minute jotting down the amount of reading you do in a month. Don't worry about detail, just go for ballpark guesses. For the purpose of this exercise, we'll just consider books: break them down into novels, business books and other nonfiction. Just estimate the number of books in each category you get through in a month.

Reading books is fundamental to creativity and knowledge enhancement, yet few of us give it enough time. Consider the balance you have. Should you take on another business book a month? Should you double your fiction intake? Check in your diary for opportunities to do a little more reading – and stick to it.

Feedback Everyone could read more, and 'I just haven't got time' simply isn't an acceptable excuse. All that says is you've got bad time management. Everyone should be able to make time for at least one book in each category a month – most of us many more. Consider time when you could sensibly read. On trains and planes. In your lunchtime. In the evening instead of watching TV. In bed. It might be that you read plenty, but you never read fiction. In that case, you are in danger of having an unbalanced diet. Fiction, especially speculative fiction, is a great way of stretching your imagination. Don't ignore it. Similarly, don't stick to your specialist areas of nonfiction. Explore chaos theory or music to get new insights.

Outcome Reading a little more is one of the simplest ways of contributing to your knowledge and creativity. Much creativity comes from spotting something in a totally different field that is relevant to your requirement: reading a wide range of topics is the best way to achieve this. Everyone can manage it.

Variations For specifics on finding books, see Chapter 6.

Knowledge	✪✪✪✪
Memory	✪
Creativity	✪✪✪✪
Fun	✪✪✪✪

5.24 Spinning knowledge

Preparation Familiarize yourself with the basics of finding things on the Web.
Running time 10 minutes.
Resources Access to the World Wide Web.
Frequency Once.

Choose a subject that you know very little about. It should be something quite specific without requiring heavy technical knowledge – like rose pruning or the basics of how a compact disk works. Using the World Wide Web, see how much you can find out about the subject in 10 minutes. You don't need to absorb everything, but try to make sure that you know where to get back to information that is particularly relevant. If you don't know much about the Web, enter your topic in the AltaVista search engine (http://www.altavista.com).

Feedback The volume of information you can amass this way is quite frightening – in fact part of the skill of using the Web is being able to filter down from a huge number of possible sources to the information you want. It's also worth bearing in mind that the Web isn't always the best source of information. If you want, for example, something you might find in a dictionary or an encyclopedia you might be better with a book or a CD-ROM – but for most topics the Web is superb.

Outcome Knowledge is dependent on being able to get hold of the right information quickly when you need it. Increasingly, the World Wide Web is the easiest way to do this. If you aren't particularly hot at finding information on the Web, see Chapter 6 for information on the book *Mining the Internet*. Using the Internet well is a non-optional skill for knowledge managers.

Variations It is easy to lose track of time when using the Web. Consider using a kitchen timer to give you a warning when 10 minutes is up.

Knowledge	✪✪✪✪
Memory	✪
Creativity	✪✪
Fun	✪✪

5.25 Going down

Preparation None.
Running time Five minutes.
Resources None.
Frequency Once.

You may have heard this problem before. Don't stop reading, we are going beyond the usual conclusion. Every morning a man gets into the lift (elevator) on the floor of the high rise block he lives in and rides down to ground level. Every evening he comes home, gets in the lift, rides up to the tenth floor (four below his own), gets out and walks the rest of the way. Why?

If you haven't heard it before, think about it for a while before reading on.

Now an extra piece of information. The man was easily tall enough to reach every button in the lift. Think about the problem some more.

Feedback Last chance to think. There are many solutions. The man could want a little exercise and four floors of stairs are enough. He might suspect his wife of adultery and want to surprise her. He could stop off at a friend's four floors below for a drink each evening. And so on. But what if he actually has to get out rather than wants to – surely the conventional solution (the man is too short to reach) is now the only one? No. The higher lift buttons could be broken. The owners of the building could charge for each floor you ride up. He only has a 10-floor ticket, so he has to walk the rest. Or there is building work going on in the afternoon which restricts the travel of the lift. Feel like arguing with these solutions? The traditional solution is equally frail – whenever there is someone else in the lift he can get to the right floor.

Outcome There are two issues here. The first is that a late arriving piece of information can totally change our knowledge base – and it's difficult to give up an established position. The second is to observe just how many solutions there are – and how conditions can be used to question any idea, however valid.

Variations Whenever you come across puzzles like this, look for alternative solutions.

Knowledge	✪✪✪
Memory	✪✪
Creativity	✪✪✪✪
Fun	✪✪✪

5.26 The little black book

Preparation None.
Running time Five minutes.
Resources Address book.
Frequency Weekly.

Once a week, spend five minutes keeping your address book up to date. Add new business cards. Note any contacts you have made. Try to put in keyword information about the contact, not just bare name and address. Get an e-mail address if possible. Prune out a few people who aren't needed any more.

To do this, you need an address book in the first place. The best type is an electronic one on a PC, as you can have as many entries as you like (usually), you can add and delete at will, letting the system sort out the alphabetical order, you can search on anything in the book and you can use categories to lump people together.

Feedback Remember the hackneyed saying, 'It's not what you know, but who you know'. If knowledge is the art of knowing, it's not surprising that managing who you know is valuable to your personal knowledge management. Of course, the saying implies that it doesn't matter how clever you are, you can still be overcome by influence and corruption. But there's also a positive side to it. If you accept that you can't know everything (a wise step), you will sometimes need to look to others for help, support and advice. With an up-to-date little black book, containing enough keywords to pull out the right people, you have an instant knowledge support network.

Outcome Address books naturally grow out of date. By allocating a small amount of time on a regular basis (best to put it in your diary), you can ensure that this valuable knowledge resource remains current.

Variations The essentials for knowledge support are telephone and e-mail, because there is often an immediacy that can't wait for the post. A specific variant is your little black book of Web sites. If the Web is to be a significant knowledge resource (see *Spinning knowledge*, 5.24) you will need to keep track of important sites.

Knowledge	✪✪✪✪
Memory	✪
Creativity	✪
Fun	✪

5.27 We ask the questions

Preparation *On the box*, 5.1.
Running time 10 minutes.
Resources Notepad.
Frequency Once.

It's not essential, but you might like to try *On the box* before performing this exercise. Imagine that you had to interview someone. He is the chairman of a toy company. One of his products has recently proved dangerous, and there is evidence that the company knew about the dangers for at least a year before the toys were withdrawn.

Spend five minutes putting together an interview plan. What question are you going to open with? What potential questions might you go on to ask? Get a plan together before reading more.

Now imagine that he starts to answer your first question, then changes tack. He says that the toys were not withdrawn at the orders of the government. He has documentary evidence to prove this, and his company is the victim of a government conspiracy. What question would you ask immediately? How would you reform your interview plan during his answer?

Feedback Interviewing skills are essential for knowledge management. A good interview plan needs a clear opening question, then a series of other questions forming potential directions that can be steered and reformed by the response from the interviewee. Flexible notation, like mind mapping (see 5.12) is a great help here. Be prepared for something totally unexpected. We've all heard interviewers floundering on with their original agenda when everything has changed. A good way to cope is to recap the unexpected statement as a question to give you time to reformulate your plan. If the chairman was asked, 'Are you really saying the government made you do this?' it would keep the flow going while you regrouped.

Outcome Even if you don't interview formally, informal interviewing will be part of your knowledge gathering skills. If you can hone these skills you will have a better chance of gaining expertise.

Variations Do the theoretical exercise even if you have an interview coming up soon – but make sure you try out the technique for real as soon as possible.

Knowledge	✪✪✪✪
Memory	✪
Creativity	✪✪
Fun	✪✪

5.28 Follow the finger

Preparation None.
Running time 10 minutes.
Resources None.
Frequency Once.

You already know how to read, so there is no more to learn, right? Wrong. In this exercise you will use a visual guide to speed up your reading. This is nothing new. You used one when you first began reading – your finger. In fact, the guide can still be your finger, or the end of a pen or pencil – any pointer you are comfortable holding while reading. There's one big difference, though. Instead of pointing at each word in turn, run the guide smoothly along under the text. Start at your habitual reading rate, then notch up the speed. You will find a marked acceleration over a short period of practice.

When you are comfortable with the guide, try a different method. Instead of moving the guide along the text, move it down the centre of the page. It is possible to pick up the meaning of whole lines of text by interpolation. You can't read every word this way, but it is a highly efficient way of skimming. The technique takes a little longer to get the hang of, but is well worth acquiring.

Feedback Using a visual guide might make you feel uncomfortable. After all, you did this at age five. Then, though, the finger followed the speed with which you could recognize words. Now the guide leads your eyes. Because of infantile associations, you may find a pencil end less embarrassing than a finger.

Outcome These complementary techniques will increase your speed of detailed reading and your skimming speed. The simple guide alone can increase reading speeds by between 50 and 100 per cent. This can be used to absorb more material or to have longer to make something out of the results – to turn information into knowledge.

Variations If you find difficulty reading when skimming the guide down the middle of the page, try different movements – curving or diagonal transitions across the page.

Knowledge	✪✪✪✪
Memory	✪
Creativity	✪✪
Fun	✪

5.29 On the edge

Preparation None.
Running time 10 minutes.
Resources Notepad.
Frequency Regularly.

Choose an area of personal knowledge – a field in which you consider yourself something of an expert. The aim of this exercise is to test the limits of your knowledge, filling out the gaps. Spend a couple of minutes drawing out a keyword map of what you know (if you aren't familiar with mapping, see *Surveying your mind*, 5.12, first).

Now highlight some aspects of your map. Is there knowledge you know is quite old in a fast changing area? Highlight it. Where are the edges of your knowledge? What parts of it are fuzzy, or border into a different discipline you don't know about, or go into more technical detail than you can handle?

Pull out the highlighted areas onto a separate sheet of paper.

Feedback The detail of widening your knowledge isn't an instant activity, but this exercise has produced an action list for further investigation. At the very least you should check that your ageing knowledge isn't past its sell by date – in some areas knowledge has a very short shelf life. You may also like to push the boundaries – to expand into some of those fringe areas. The aim isn't to make you a know-it-all, but to be sure of the solidity of your essential knowledge, which often requires a grounding in surrounding areas even if you haven't deep expertise.

Outcome You should get an internally driven plan for sharpening up your knowledge in a key area. There will, of course, be external sources of need too, which are covered in other exercises.

Variations Most of us have several areas of knowledge, but keep the exercise focused on a single subject, and have another go another time for a different area. Consider making this a regular process – the frequency depends on how quickly your knowledge area changes.

Knowledge	✪✪✪✪
Memory	✪✪✪
Creativity	✪
Fun	✪✪

5.30 Quick on the draw

Preparation None.
Running time 10 minutes.
Resources Notepad.
Frequency Once.

Most of us are convinced that we are bad at drawing. But try this exercise before you dismiss your own abilities.

Without anything to look at, draw a picture of a house with a person and a car outside it. Don't spend more than a couple of minutes over it. Put that picture aside. Now take a toy or a cartoon-style picture (rather than a photograph) and draw a copy of it. Don't use a clever technique like squaring off the paper, and try to draw fluidly rather than in minute detail. If things start going horribly wrong, throw the picture away and start again.

Feedback You will probably find you were much better at copying than at producing the first drawing. Most adults' drawings of the car, the house and the child don't differ much from a five-year-old's. How is it possible that your drawing skills improved so much between the two pictures? After all, there's nothing too challenging about a car or a house. In fact, we are mostly much better at drawing than we allow – but we are limited by our ability to visualize and by the certainty that we 'can't draw'. A number of other exercises in this book help with visualization. Here, we are just aiming for an understanding of a classic limitation of creativity.

Outcome This exercise isn't designed to turn you into an artist, although you may well find you can draw a lot better than you thought. Instead it should put across the importance of visualization and give a potential boost to your creativity.

Variations Given your new-found abilities, try copying a photograph of a person. The result is usually much more like a real person than your visualized person, but still varies hugely from the original. Why is that? What could you do differently? If you want to pursue drawing further, see *Drawing on the Right Side of Your Brain* in Chapter 6.

Knowledge	✪✪✪
Memory	✪
Creativity	✪✪✪✪
Fun	✪✪

5.31 Story time

Preparation Find a book of short stories.
Running time 30 minutes.
Resources Short story.
Frequency Once.

Reading a short story can be more than just entertainment – done the right way it can enhance your creativity. Find a brief short story (no more than five or six pages). It should be challenging, whether it's science fiction or just about an extreme circumstance – it shouldn't be everyday. Read the story through.

Now spend a few minutes thinking about the story. What did the author do and say that was unexpected, or that you don't normally encounter in real life? What sort of point(s) of view does the story use? Try to get below the surface of the story and into the mind of the writer.

Feedback In putting together a story (you can have a go yourself in *Scribbling,* 5.62), the writer suspends reality and looks at life differently. This is essential for creativity. If you are having difficulty finding an appropriate story, try *Imagination Engineering* (see page 107), a textbook on creativity that ends each chapter with a short story chosen for this purpose. How else would you describe a story written from the point of view of a nasturtium, or a story that describes itself being written backwards from the last word to the first? It's important to stress the need for unusual fiction. Great literature often portrays very ordinary circumstances. Feel free to read that as well, but this exercise needs something more – that glimpse of a different world that will inspire a new viewpoint in the reader.

Outcome Familiarizing yourself with the way a writer suspends reality and devises a fictional world with an alternative viewpoint is excellent preparation for being more creative.

Variations Although this is labelled a one-off exercise, you can get plenty more value by keeping up your fiction reading. If you see reading as part of your lifetime learning, rather than just entertainment, perhaps you can give it a higher priority. A regular diet of unusual fiction, will keep your creativity on the bubble.

Knowledge	✪
Memory	✪
Creativity	✪✪✪✪
Fun	✪✪✪✪

5.32 Leaf mould

Preparation None.
Running time Five minutes.
Resources A tree leaf.
Frequency Once.

Get hold of a reasonably broad tree leaf. Find somewhere comfortable and sit down. You are going to be asked to do a number of things with the leaf. Read the first short sentence, do it, then come back and take on the next requirement. Try to focus as much as possible on one activity at a time.

1. Look at the leaf in a general way: turn it over in your hand and get a feel for it.
2. Look closely at the leaf. Examine the fine detail. Look at the veins, the edges of the leaf, the way it joins on to the stem and so on.
3. Think into the leaf. What is under the surface? It doesn't matter if your biology is weak, just imagine what goes together to make up the leaf.
4. Think from the leaf back to the tree. How would the leaf sit on the tree? What would surround it? How would the light and the air play around it?
5. Finally, gently tear the leaf. Try to feel the individual parts of the leaf resisting your pressure. Look at the torn edge: how does it differ from the natural edges?

Feedback When we are young we look at everything with fascination, but as we grow older habit and experience dulls that fascination. We all know that leaves are common and uninspiring – any garden or park is full of the things. Yet they are complex, intriguing objects.

Outcome Getting back a little of the naïve interest of childhood is a major step both for knowledge management and creativity. A child's creativity depends on not 'knowing' everything – taking a moment to look at a leaf reveals how much we usually take for granted. Our 'knowing' is very limited indeed.

Variations Take the time to look at other 'everyday' things more closely. You can't do it all the time, but every now and then it's a wonderful exercise.

Knowledge	✪✪✪✪
Memory	✪
Creativity	✪✪✪✪
Fun	✪✪✪

5.33 Car and goats

Preparation None.
Running time 10 minutes.
Resources None.
Frequency Oncc.

Here's a problem to tax your creative thinking. You are a game show contestant and reach the final round. The game is simple. The host shows you three doors. Behind one is a sports car. Behind the other two are goats. You choose a door, and win whatever is behind it.

You choose a door. Before you open it, the host (who knows what is behind every door) opens one of the other doors and shows you a goat. She now gives you the chance to stick with the door you first chose or to change your choice. What should you do? Stick, change – or does it not matter what you do?

Feedback If you haven't already got an answer, jot one down now. When I perform this exercise with a group, I conduct a survey at this point. Most say it doesn't matter, some say stick, a few say move. Only the few are correct. You double your chances of winning by changing. This does not seem logical. After all, of the remaining doors one is a car and one is a goat. Surely there's a 50-50 chance? The reasoning is this; initially, you have a one-in-three chance of guessing the correct door, so there's a two-in-three chance that the car is behind one of the others. The host shows you one of the other doors it isn't behind, but there's still a two-in-three chance you guessed wrong. If that doesn't make sense, read it a few more times. Don't worry if it still seems crazy – when this puzzle was first published there were angry letters from professors denying the truth of it. But you can prove it with a computer – changing is the right thing to do.

Outcome Here's a situation where common sense is outraged: it shows how intuition should be treated carefully.

Variations If you can't accept the result, let it simmer for a few days, then look at it again.

Knowledge	✪✪
Memory	✪
Creativity	✪✪✪✪
Fun	✪✪✪

5.34 Found story

Preparation None.
Running time 10 minutes.
Resources Notepad.
Frequency Once.

Spend a couple of minutes taking a walk outside (or around a building if outside isn't practical). Find an object you can take back to a quiet place. It can be anything – just something portable that catches your eye.

Now take a minute to think of a context for this object. It should be something totally incongruous. Think of the object in a sensationalist newspaper headline. For example it might be 'the nutcrackers from outer space', or 'the wallet that ate my hamster', or 'my personal organizer is having a baby'.

Finally take five minutes to write a short story on this theme. It should take the context entirely seriously. It can be in the form of a newspaper article or a narrative. Don't spend ages thinking about it – force yourself to write, whatever drivel you produce.

Feedback Despite appearances, this isn't about creative writing – it's the thought process that's important, not the writing. Creativity is all about generating new ideas and concepts which somehow don't quite fit with current thinking. At a later date they will be absorbed into the mainstream, but initially they will often seem odd. The companion book, *Instant Creativity*, is full of techniques to help to stimulate this sort of idea generation. Yet before you can make the mental leaps prompted by a technique, you need the ability to detach yourself from a conventional train of thought. Exercises like this are designed to do just that.

Outcome By chipping away at your normal, blinkered view of the world, this technique improves your capability to be creative.

Variations There are almost an infinite number of contexts in which you can put any object. These can range from the mundane ('the stone that wasn't there yesterday'), to the unusual ('the stone that got a degree from Cambridge'). It's a good idea to keep the context unusual, because that helps to force a creative viewpoint.

Knowledge	✪✪
Memory	✪
Creativity	✪✪✪✪
Fun	✪✪✪

5.35 Remember, remember

Preparation None.
Running time Five minutes.
Resources Notepad.
Frequency Once.

Spend a couple of minutes assessing how you remember things. Start with the short-term. What do you do if you need to remember a telephone number between looking it up and dialling it? How do you remember a message from the phone? How do you remember a task you need to handle today? Then work through some typical medium-term items. Something you need to remember for a week, a few weeks, a few months. Finally, look at how you fix things into your long-term memory.

Look for any weaknesses in your approach. Sometimes, the methods we use actually get in the way. For example, using a yellow sticky note to remember a single urgent action is fine. Once your PC screen or desk is covered in sticky notes, it becomes a sure way of forgetting things. Putting something in a task list is great – as long as you look at the task list. Electronic lists can help by flagging up timed alerts.

Feedback Look at using memory techniques like *Number rhymes*, 5.22, to fix a phone number in place for a few minutes. To get something fixed long-term, you will need review – see *One more time*, 5.15. But the important thing here is to ensure that the mechanisms that support your memory help rather than hinder. There is considerable overlap between some aspects of memory and time management (see *Instant Time Management* in the Kogan Page Instant series). This may seem odd, as time management is often regarded as a mechanical, limiting process, but makes sense if you approach it as a way to remove the need to remember what you should be doing.

Outcome Memory seems a very natural thing, but it's only by checking out your approach and refining it that you will get the best out of it.

Variations Take a hint from SWOT analysis, and as well as looking for the weaknesses in your memory strategy, look at the strengths, the opportunities and the threats.

Knowledge	✪✪
Memory	✪✪✪✪
Creativity	✪
Fun	✪✪

5.36 Life saver

Preparation None.
Running time Five minutes.
Resources None.
Frequency Once.

A little problem to consider. You are locked in a cell. It has a circular floor, five metres in diameter, and smooth concrete walls four metres high. In the centre of the floor is a hole, 10 cm deep. At the bottom of the hole is a smooth wooden ball which drops easily into the hole, but is only a little smaller in diameter than the hole itself. You have been stripped and have nothing about your person. You are given three conventional wire paperclips. You will only be allowed out of the cell if you can get the ball out of the hole. What do you do?

Feedback If you haven't got a solution, keep trying for a little longer. Last chance to try. There's a natural tendency to assume that since you are only given one tool, there must be some way of using it. Unfortunately, this assumption is flawed. Just because you are given something, you don't have to use it. The paperclips aren't really very helpful. However, you do have a way of getting the ball out of the hole. After all, wooden balls float, so all you have to is get some liquid into the hole: the rest of the solution is left to your imagination.

Outcome Sometimes attempting to use everything that has been provided in coming up with a solution to a problem, or in making a decision based on knowledge, can be a positive block to a solution. This problem demonstrates how it is sometimes useful to drop some of the 'given' input to see what else is available.

Variations This doesn't say you need always ignore the tools you're given, but that giving some consideration to how things would work without them can be valuable. Try applying this thinking to various everyday problems and situations where tools are employed.

Knowledge	✪✪✪
Memory	✪
Creativity	✪✪✪✪
Fun	✪✪✪

5.37 Get a laugh

Preparation Get hold of a business humour book.
Running time 15 minutes.
Resources Book.
Frequency Several times a year.

Humour is one of the vital components of creativity. Almost all humour involves taking the familiar and looking at it in a different way – the core of creative inspiration. One of the best ways to enhance your creativity around a business theme is to indulge in some business humour. Get hold of a humorous business book – Scott Adams' *Dilbert* books or Robert Townsend's *Up The Organization* series are a good start. On a regular basis, make sure that you read a chunk of one of these books. It may well be, once you are started, that you find you want to read the whole book. If so, don't fight it.

Feedback Reading in the workplace is frowned upon, even when the subject is serious business texts, so having a funny book on your desk in working hours may not be a good move for your career prospects. It ought to be – after all, this is probably more educational than the course that wastes much more of your time – but company culture is unlikely to support it. That being the case, take the pragmatic view and read it in your lunchtime, or out of business hours.

Outcome The great thing about a business humour book is that you win on several counts. It is entertaining in its own right. It exposes you to a creative view of the business world, enhancing your own potential creativity, and it points out very specific flaws in business practice that you can learn from. Not bad for one book.

Variations For specifics on finding humorous business books, see Chapter 6.

Knowledge	✪✪✪
Memory	✪
Creativity	✪✪✪✪
Fun	✪✪✪✪

5.38 Rapt concentration

Preparation None.
Running time Five minutes.
Resources A quiet place.
Frequency Several times.

Concentration is a great gift – but it is something we are all bad at. This extremely simple exercise will help to boost your powers of concentration.

Find yourself a quiet place where you can have five minutes without distraction. Sit quietly and take a few slow breaths. Now begin to count up from one in your head. Continue to do so as long as you can concentrate purely on the numbers without anything else – anything – creeping into your thoughts.

It won't take long the first time. Repeat a number of times, trying to increase your concentration span.

Feedback In fact it's hardly ever possible to get past 10 at a first go. Some thought, however small, will usually manage to creep in. It won't stop you counting – you will continue on automatic pilot, but the numbers will have lost your concentration. You may find you need to repeat this exercise on a number of occasions to get any significant improvement.

Outcome Often we don't need to give total concentration to what we are doing, and some great ideas can come out of thoughts that take place in the background (see *Unconscious creativity*, 5.61). However, there are occasions when total focus is intensely useful to carry out a critical action. What's more, simple awareness of the impracticality of pure concentration will be of value – for instance, next time you have to give a presentation.

Variations Counting is the simplest way of performing this exercise, but you can also perform it by listening to music, and trying to concentrate solely on the notes being played, or by looking at a simple set of abstract shapes and only thinking about the shapes themselves.

Knowledge	✪✪
Memory	✪✪✪
Creativity	✪✪✪
Fun	✪✪

5.39 Material gains

Preparation None.
Running time Five minutes.
Resources Notepad.
Frequency Once.

Think of a broad area of manufacturing, where the materials used are fairly constant. For example, it might be cars (steel), planes (lightweight metals), office buildings (glass and concrete) or crockery (clay). Note down the manufacturing area at the top of the page of your notepad. Below it put four circles. In the first, put the material(s) you are familiar with. In each of the others, put a totally different material. For example, for cars the materials might be water, carpet and rubber.

In the remainder of the time, let your eyes skim over the materials and slot in any thoughts you have below on the positive implications of making this product from the material. Don't try to be systematic and work through one of each, just let the ideas flow. Don't link implications to practicalities. For instance, a positive implication of making cars out of water is that they'd be easy to park – it doesn't matter how it would work.

Feedback You might find it difficult to start with to stay positive. After all, a car made from water is ludicrous. Yet all creative ideas sound crazy to start with. You often need a change of viewpoint and a refinement of the idea before it becomes useful. The trouble is, we tend to squash them too early. This enforced positiveness will help to restrain your natural tendencies.

Outcome This is also very good practice for thinking differently about very solid, very everyday things – an essential for creativity.

Variations Here we are using this approach to broaden your creative thinking. However, this technique could be used as a practical creativity technique for specific purposes. Thinking of the implications of building a car out of water, carpet and rubber – and what you would have to do to make them work – would be an excellent way to develop a new car (out of conventional materials) that had some genuinely new features.

Knowledge	✪✪
Memory	✪
Creativity	✪✪✪✪
Fun	✪✪✪✪

5.40 Twisters

Preparation None.
Running time Five minutes.
Resources None.
Frequency Once.

Attempt an answer to each of these three short puzzles before moving on to the feedback section.

- What game (with four letters) starts with a T, originated in Scotland and is played outdoors?
- Pandas are endangered, but they have an aid to survival that is totally unique to their species. What is it?
- Why were so many great composers German?

Feedback Don't go any further until you've attempted some sort of answer to each. Last chance to consider your answer. The answers are: golf (it starts with a tee); baby pandas; because they were born in Germany. Each of these twisters depends on taking something about the information you are given and using it in a way that you don't expect. Once you've groaned at the answers (if you hadn't already guessed them), take a minute to examine what was happening.

Outcome Creativity is all about seeing the world in a different way, or coming at a problem from a different direction. These puzzles work in exactly the same way. By practising this sort of puzzle, you have a much better chance of coming up with creative ideas. This is also an effective lesson for knowledge management. In each case, you knew the answer – it was the question you didn't understand. It emphasizes the need for careful questioning when you are acquiring knowledge.

Variations Get hold of a book of this sort of puzzle and practise the type of thinking required. You may also find cryptic crossword puzzles give the same kind of exercise.

Knowledge	✪✪✪
Memory	✪
Creativity	✪✪✪✪
Fun	✪✪✪

5.41 Mapping for memory

Preparation *Surveying your mind*, 5.12.
Running time 10 minutes.
Resources Notepad; coloured pens or pencils.
Frequency Oncc.

In *Surveying your mind*, we looked at taking notes more flexibly and memorably than with conventional text. This is enough if your only aim is to capture and structure information. But if your intention is to remember it, there are ways to enhance the map. Usually this involves redrawing. Take an existing mind map, or quickly draw one for practice. There are three aims.

- Make sure the structure is the best for your information. You may need more space for one of the topics, or it might have been better to have a different branch heading. Restructure the map if necessary.
- Bring in colour. Unless you are colour blind, colour helps retention of information. Either write each branch and its text in a different colour or colour in the lines of each branch. Make sure the colours are legible.
- Bring in imagery. Put your branch headings in 3D boxes. Draw icons to illustrate the concepts. If information on separate branches needs linking, use fancy curved arrows.

Feedback There are two problems with this technique. One is bothering to do it. It isn't necessary every time you take notes, only when you need to remember the detail. By focusing it on these occasions it can be less of a problem. Secondly, it is reminiscent of that irritating person at school who always underlined words in different colours and was generally a bit of a pain. This is different – the only thing you are showing off to is your memory.

Outcome Restructuring information that needs to be recalled will give a significant boost to your memory. Just the action of redrawing also helps to revise the topic.

Variations How you work over your map is up to you. The important things are that the artwork doesn't obscure the message, and that the colour and imagery help to reinforce the information.

Knowledge	✪✪✪
Memory	✪✪✪✪
Creativity	✪✪
Fun	✪✪

5.42 Fact quest

Preparation None.
Running time 10 minutes.
Resources Whatever reference facilities you normally use.
Frequency Once.

There are many sources of information that can expand your knowledge and excite your creativity. This exercise focuses on the knowledge library at your fingertips. Think for a moment of your surroundings at work. What sources of information are there to hand – books, CDs, intranet and Internet, company databases, magazines and newspapers? Jot them down. Think of your environment at home, too. Jot down what is available there. Try your normal reference facilities to come up with answers to these questions. Allow no more than 10 minutes.

- Napoleon Bonaparte's birthday.
- The atomic weight of caesium.
- What are the actual words of that well-known quote about 'For whom the bell tolls' – and who wrote it?
- A definition of prelibation.
- Yesterday's share price for British Airways.
- The name of the chief executive of Ford UK.
- The type of laser used in a laser printer.

Feedback Don't worry if you wouldn't normally want to know half these things, just find them out. If your resources include the Internet, that's great, but be a little careful about using the World Wide Web for getting hold of specific facts. Not only will you sometimes come to a wrong answer, it often isn't the best way to come to a pure fact. See the book, *Mining the Internet*, described in Chapter 6 for more on using the Internet safely for research.

Outcome Good knowledge skills include the ability to get hold of facts – and you never know just what those facts are going to be. This exercise tests your resources.

Variations Feel free to try out different types of fact beyond the categories I've listed here. You might like to get someone else in your own area of speciality to put together a fact list. But don't miss this more general exercise – you never know just what facts you might need.

Knowledge	✪✪✪✪
Memory	✪
Creativity	✪✪
Fun	✪✪✪

5.43 Versatile coat hangers

Preparation None.
Running time Five minutes.
Resources Notepad.
Frequency Once.

Spend two minutes jotting down everything you can do with a coat hanger. Don't go into detail, just a set of bullet-point headings.

Now spend another two minutes noting everything you can't do with a coat hanger.

Look at the two lists. It's usually easier to come up with more things you can't do than things you can. This isn't surprising when you consider what a very small part of 'everything' a coat hanger occupies.

Finally, pick a couple of your 'can't' entries and turn them around. Assume that you can do absolutely anything with a coat hanger. How can you make this use possible? You might not succeed, but you will be surprised how often it is possible.

Feedback I often use this exercise in creativity seminars, and usually manage to defeat most attempts at finding an impossible use. In finding things you can't do, you are limited by your own assumptions. For example, it was never stated that the coat hanger was a wire one, or that you couldn't process it in some way. So for instance, if the challenge is to drink it, the coat hanger could be made of ice – just melt it and drink it. Another popular one is to have sex with it: luckily, people make excellent coat hangers. About the only use I normally concede defeat on is using it as an effective car aerial.

Outcome The more you practise overcoming your personal restraints on creativity, the better you will be at developing creative solutions.

Variations If you had trouble disproving your negative arguments, try again now you realize that the coat hanger can be made of anything, processed in any way, human, animal, vegetable, mineral – the choice is yours.

Knowledge	✪✪
Memory	✪
Creativity	✪✪✪✪
Fun	✪✪✪

5.44 Game theory

Preparation Obtain a computer adventure game.
Running time 30 minutes.
Resources Computer.
Frequency Several times.

Get hold of a computer-based adventure game. If you aren't sure what this is, talk to a teenager or ask at your local computer games shop. Glance through the instructions, but don't worry too much about them. Launch into the game and spend around half an hour exploring it. Don't spend much longer, unless you want to for entertainment. But come back to the game a number of times.

Feedback It may seem strange to recommend as a practical exercise what many would regard as an adolescent pastime, but an adventure game contains two prime challenges. To succeed in such a game, you need to build knowledge of your environment and solve puzzles. Because the environment is artificial, the knowledge is 'pure' – it isn't something you can already have gathered elsewhere, so the practical experience is guaranteed to be valuable. Similarly, the puzzles are specifically designed to require creative solutions. In the companion book, *Instant Creativity*, adventure games are recommended as a way of changing the viewpoint. In that case, we suggested using 'walkthroughs' to guide you through the puzzles, as the aim was to get you into a different frame of mind. Here, the aim is to improve your knowledge development and creativity, so you should try to solve the puzzles and find your way around without help.

Outcome Few activities combine more effective practice at two of the prime aspects of brain power.

Variations This is definitely one to use outside your conventional working environment, as even the most enlightened management is liable to raise an eyebrow if this is described as knowledge management and creativity training.

Knowledge	✪✪✪✪
Memory	✪✪
Creativity	✪✪✪✪
Fun	✪✪✪✪

5.45 Technical creativity

Preparation A problem statement.
Running time 10 minutes.
Resources Notepad.
Frequency Once.

For this exercise we need a problem statement or idea requirement. It needn't be a real problem, but it doesn't do any harm if it is. State the problem in a single sentence beginning 'How to'. For instance, 'How to increase throughput of the production line'.

Turn a piece of paper on its side and write the problem statement across the middle of the page. Ring the key words in the sentence. In this case they would be 'increase', 'throughput' and 'production line'. From each of these ringed words or phrases, draw lines with alternatives, opposites, or just things they make you think of. For instance, 'increase' could generate 'decrease', 'throughput' could generate 'catflap' and 'production line' could generate 'chorus line'. Each ringed word will normally generate several alternatives.

Finally, try using different words in the problem statement. What might you do to decrease the catflap of the production line, or increase the throughput of the chorus line? Don't worry if the result sounds nonsensical – think of the possibilities. What does it imply for your problem? Some catflaps, for example, are one-way doors. Are there one-way parts of the production line which could be reversed to increase productivity?

Feedback There are many techniques for generating ideas and solving problems. They aren't the main thrust of this book – if you want to find many more, see the companion title, *Instant Creativity*. However, using creativity techniques is a reliable way to increase your personal creativity, so this one, specially devised for this book, has been included.

Outcome The practical outcome of using a technique like this is to generate a new idea or to solve a problem. Here we are more interested in their value in encouraging a different way of looking at the world, and hence a more creative frame of mind.

Variations See Chapter 6 for other books on creativity techniques.

Knowledge	✪✪
Memory	✪
Creativity	✪✪✪✪
Fun	✪✪

5.46 Stolen thoughts

Preparation A problem or idea requirement.
Running time 10 minutes.
Resources Notepad.
Frequency Once.

Ideally, start this exercise with a problem or idea requirement in mind. If you haven't anything significant right now, use an artificial problem like, 'How to design a totally new type of computer software', or 'How to choose a new office chair for our company'.

Spend a few minutes thinking who you could steal an idea or a solution from. Who has similar problems? Who has different problems that you could learn from? Who has already gone through this decision process? Who has tried what you will have to try? Is there any publication or journal that might cover it?

Next spend a few minutes thinking about how you would obtain information on what other people have done.

If you've got time and opportunity, take the final step and get hold of some information.

Feedback There is a natural tendency to think that copying what other people do is wrong. A number of factors contribute to this. It is frowned upon at school. There are legal worries (but remember, you can't copyright an idea). It is somehow unprofessional. Rubbish. It may be true that parrot-like copying won't get you very far, but it is simply ludicrous to ignore the effort other people have put into a decision or finding out information. Use them as a stepping stone. Don't copy slavishly, but always take external input.

Outcome 'Not invented here' is the enemy of creativity. Unfortunately, for too long, managers have assumed that fighting 'not invented here' meant that nothing good can be invented here. That just isn't logical. But combining a knowledge of what has worked for other people with your own circumstances, experience and creativity is a real recipe for success.

Variations You can invert this exercise by looking at what you shouldn't copy from other people, itself very enlightening.

Knowledge	✪✪✪✪
Memory	✪
Creativity	✪✪✪✪
Fun	✪✪

5.47 Broken CD

Preparation Invent scenario.
Running time Five minutes.
Resources A stooge.
Frequency Once.

Imagine a situation in which you have to complain about something. Persuade a colleague to act as a stooge in trying out this scenario. They are to counter your request. For example, you could be taking back a broken product and demanding a replacement, or asking for a refund in a restaurant. This is a different approach to the *Broken record technique*, 5.2. Think of at least half a dozen different ways of asking the same thing. They should be as different as possible without actually varying the outcome. Instead of repeatedly asking the same thing, run round your different phrasing. Probe the other person for aspects of the question that they don't understand.

Feedback Sometimes when you are trying to gain knowledge you will be resisted. This could be for three reasons – because the person doesn't know, because he or she simply doesn't want to tell you, or because he or she doesn't understand your question. This exercise gives some practice in dealing with the third possibility, with elements of the second thrown in for good measure. Make sure that you keep your repeated requests low key and friendly. Nod, agree, say 'Yes, I see', to the other person's reasons for not coming up with the goods – then ask a different way. This technique is best used face to face; it's too easy for the other person to just put the phone down. If you find it very difficult, practise some more – it becomes relatively easy and even enjoyable.

Outcome It is surprising how often this technique will whittle away resistance and get a result, and it can be less irritating than the pure broken record technique.

Variations If there is a genuine circumstance when you can practise the technique, so much the better. This could either be in the sort of scenario used here (complaint), or when you are trying to get information from reluctant source.

Knowledge	✪✪✪✪
Memory	✪
Creativity	✪
Fun	✪✪

5.48 The bookshop raid

Preparation Find a good bookshop.
Running time 30 minutes.
Resources Notepad.
Frequency Once.

Find yourself a good bookshop – not a newsagent with a few books. Take yourself up to the business section with a notebook. You are going to indulge in some potential knowledge acquisition. There are definitely some books in there which will help you. Normally you are dependent on recommendation to hit on something appropriate – this time it's going to be proactive.

Work from one end of the section to the other. Ignore the categories within the section – few parts of a bookshop are more confusingly organized than the business section. And that was before other browsers mixed it up. Don't worry if you aren't interested in 'human resources' or 'marketing' – that's just guesswork on the part of the bookshop staff.

Run through the titles, pulling books that sound vaguely interesting. Check the back cover blurb, the contents and the first few pages. Does this book look as if the subject matter will help you? Does the approach appeal? Both are equally important. If so, jot down the details.

Feedback It's all too easy to have your personal knowledge development blinkered by the recommendations of others. Recommendations are very valuable, but sometimes it's a good idea to take a little time to go out and look for yourself. It may seem that business books are overpriced, but compared with a course or seminar they're a bargain – they ought to be a major input to your ongoing knowledge development.

Outcome From the exercise you should have put together a business reading list. Do add important recommendations, but don't ignore the books you fancied. Buy the first couple while you are in the shop.

Variations You can take the same approach for a totally different subject – I used business as the example because this is a business book, because the sections in bookshops tend to be particularly disorganized and because it's an area where it's easy to be limited to best sellers and well-known writers.

Knowledge	✪✪✪✪
Memory	✪
Creativity	✪✪
Fun	✪✪✪

5.49 Birthday bonanza

Preparation None.
Running time Five minutes.
Resources None.
Frequency Once.

Spend a few moments thinking about this.

There are 365 days in a year (forgetting leap years for the moment). If you were offered a straight bet on whether or not there will be at least two people in a group of 30 with the same birthday (date, but not year), should you accept it?

What would you say was the break-even number of people you would need in a group so there was a 50-50 chance of having two people with the same birthday?

Feedback If you haven't already got an answer, try to jot one down now. Don't read any further. Last chance to consider your answer. Remarkably, the number is quite low. With 30 people there is a roughly 2 in 3 chance of a match – the break even number is around 23. This doesn't seem right, because the numbers involved are so large. Think of it like this. With two people, there is a 364/365th chance of not being a match. With three people, there is a 363/365th chance of the new person not having the same as the other two, but we then multiply the two together to get the chance of having no matches at all. As each extra person is added, another fraction is added to the multiplication, resulting in a surprisingly quick reduction in odds. If you don't believe it, try it in practice.

Outcome Probability (as is shown in *Car and goats*, 5.33) is often counter-intuitive. It requires just the same approach of coming at a problem from a different direction. For example, in probability, we normally calculate the chances of something happening by multiplying together the chances of the component parts not happening and subtracting from one – a sort of backward logic.

Variations Look for other opportunities to apply backward logic when presented with problems.

Knowledge	✪✪✪
Memory	✪
Creativity	✪✪✪✪
Fun	✪✪✪

5.50 Critical judgement

Preparation Get someone to write a critique of your work.
Running time 10 minutes.
Resources Helper.
Frequency Once.

Start by getting someone to write a one-page critique of some work you have done. The person ought to be a friend, and what they write should be totally private. Make sure they realize that you want constructive criticism, as hard-hitting as possible.

Without the person present, read the criticism. Don't think of any logical consequences, just examine your feelings about what has been written. Not the detail, the overall feeling it gives you. Now go back over the detail. Take each element and think of it as something you'd spotted when you were looking at your own work. There's nothing negative about it – it's just a thought you had about something you might change. Try to move criticism into an objective state. You might need to feel anger first, but then turn it into something practical.

Feedback Practically everyone hates criticism. Yet it's a powerful input to our knowledge (and self-knowledge). You might not like it, but you can understand what it's doing to you, and work around the negative feelings. Generating new ideas is an individual activity; refining those ideas is best done by a group. But it should be refinement, not shooting down ideas. Try to see criticism as someone dumping a pile of bricks outside your house that you can use to repair breaks in the walls. It might be irritating, but it's still useful. You don't have to slavishly follow the criticism, but you do need to take it seriously and push emotion out of the way.

Outcome If you can treat criticism positively and build on it, you are well on the way to enhancing your knowledge skills and polishing the results of your creativity.

Variations Don't try this one on your own. You can't irritate yourself by criticising your own work. An external view is essential, and will often add that extra something you couldn't provide alone.

Knowledge	✪✪✪✪
Memory	✪
Creativity	✪✪✪
Fun	✪✪

5.51 Number shapes

Preparation None.
Running time 10 minutes.
Resources Notepad.
Frequency Three times.

In this alternative to number rhymes, each number is associated with an image suggested by its shape. Change the image if you can think of something that works better for you:

- 1 – telegraph pole
- 2 – swan
- 3 – breasts
- 4 – folding stool
- 5 – cup (on its side)
- 6 – cherry
- 7 – scythe
- 8 – bow (tie)
- 9 – balloon
- 10 (hence 0) – Laurel and Hardy

The use is simple, but takes practice. When you want to remember a number, make up a short story in your mind linking the context of the number (eg, the person whose phone number it is) with the objects in the number shapes in the right order. Make the story as vivid and pictorial as you can. Go through the story a number of times to reinforce it.

Feedback Before you do some actual stories, try drawing the items on a pad with the number to reinforce the images. Use actual numbers you need to remember. Make the little stories as extreme, colourful, dramatic and as rude as you can to fix the memory.

Outcome This may seem a trivial technique, but it will lock practically any number into your memory. To begin with you will use the story to recall it – later the story will disappear, but the memory chain remains.

Variations This technique is an alternative to *Number rhymes*, 5.22: depending on the way your mind works you may find one or the other gives better results. Although one try may be enough to convince you, it is best to try this out three times. Make the second time later the same day as the first try. On that second attempt, do some new numbers, but also rerun the stories on the first set. Make the third try a few days later. Again, reinforce the earlier numbers. You might need to reinforce memories this way to make sure they stick.

Knowledge	✪✪
Memory	✪✪✪✪
Creativity	✪✪
Fun	✪✪

5.52 Encyclopedia dip

Preparation None.
Running time 10 minutes.
Resources Encyclopedia.
Frequency Weekly.

Every now and then, get hold of an encyclopedia. It could be a traditional paper one, but a CD-ROM-based encyclopedia is better for this exercise. Pick a letter at random, then browse through the article headings until something strikes you. It should be something that seems interesting, but is tangential to your normal areas of expertise.

Now spend 10 minutes browsing from this original point. Feel free to follow up links and digressions. Try to limit yourself strictly to 10 minutes (or at least, finishing a specific paragraph when the 10 minutes is up).

This sort of exercise can be repeated regularly with great benefit – consider putting a slot in your diary, or making it a regular lunchtime excursion, otherwise you will never get round to it.

Feedback Knowledge is a strange thing. While a lot of the basis of knowledge is very specific input, true expertise also requires a wide background awareness to be able to slot knowledge into position and to be able to branch off when new requirements come up. By having a regular trawl through uncharted information, you can help to build the level of background knowledge you have supporting your key areas.

Outcome Good foundations are essential to building a higher level of knowledge. This sort of random reading isn't an attempt to squirrel away vast amounts of information, but rather is about setting up new pathways. It is also a very valuable aid to personal creativity, as it makes it easier to see new directions from which to come at a problem.

Variations You can do something very similar by using a World Wide Web index like *Yahoo*! (see Chapter 6 for more information) and browsing down to a topic, then jumping around as the interest takes you. The Web approach will be broader, but less factual. Ideally, you should attempt both. Note, this is an entirely different exercise to *Spinning knowledge*, 5.24, where the World Wide Web is used to find specific information.

Knowledge ✪✪✪✪
Memory ✪
Creativity ✪✪✪✪
Fun ✪✪✪

5.53 Horse whispers

Preparation None.
Running time Five minutes.
Resources None.
Frequency Once.

A man stands in the centre of a large field. There are four horses in the field, one at each corner – a bay horse, a chestnut horse, a white horse and a black horse. For reasons we needn't go into, the man has to kill his horses. As he must remain at the centre of the field, the horses stay at the four corners and he is a perfect shot, how can he make sure that none of his horses remain alive by using only three bullets?

Feedback Don't go any further until you've attempted an answer. If you get one quickly, there are at least three solutions – try for another. Last chance to consider your answer. One solution is that only three of the four horses are his, so he only needs to shoot three to make sure that none of his horses remain alive. A second is that one of his horses was already dead of the terrible disease that was about to claim the others – hence his need to shoot them. A third is that the white horse was a chalk carving and had never been alive. There are more possibilities, too.

Outcome Apart from the creative exercise in coming up with a solution, there is an interesting lesson here. We are conditioned from an early age to expect a single right answer to a problem. Often in reality there are many potential right answers, something that those who depend on creativity and knowledge management forget at their peril.

Variations Can you devise any more solutions to the problem?

Knowledge	✪✪
Memory	✪
Creativity	✪✪✪✪
Fun	✪✪✪

5.54 Speed read

Preparation None.
Running time Five minutes.
Resources A book.
Frequency Several times.

In *Follow the finger*, 5.28, we look at some simple techniques using a visual guide to increase reading speed. In this exercise we provide a different approach to speed reading. Take a book and begin to 'read' it, allowing around two seconds per page. You might find something that can give a regular tick – a clock, a metronome or a PC program will help to manage this. To begin with, just let you eyes drift over the page without any conscious effort to take something in. After a number of pages, really try to take in what is on the page as you scan it.

Feedback This technique may seem bizarre, but the process is very logical. The intention is not to enable you to read books at this speed (though you may find with practice that you can take in a surprising amount), but rather to condition you to the effects of high-speed reading, so that when you read at a more normal speed it seems trivial to take things in. This has been likened to the feeling of ponderous ease we usually feel when driving on normal roads after a prolonged period on a motorway.

Outcome A few sessions of this speed scanning can make a significant contribution to speeding up your normal reading. As with *Follow the finger*, this can both increase the amount of information you can absorb in a given time and give you more time to absorb the information and integrate it into knowledge.

Variations Try different timings and see how much you can take in at a scan. For more on reading and learning, see Chapter 6.

Knowledge	✪✪✪✪
Memory	✪
Creativity	✪
Fun	✪

5.55 I never forget a face

Preparation *Name game*, 5.19.
Running time Five minutes.
Resources Some faces.
Frequency Once.

There's a subtle distinction between remembering names and remembering faces. The technique *Name game* is often enough to pin a name to a person, but sometimes you find that you have retained a set of names, but can't remember which name applies to which person. It's best to try this technique after *Name game*.

Look at the individual's face. If they have a very strong characteristic (a bald head, a huge nose), don't ignore it, but take it as part of the overall image. It won't be enough on its own, as there are plenty more people with a similar characteristic. Expand your view to take in the whole person if possible. Now superimpose the image you have generated for their name on that person. Imagine them incorporating the image, or doing something unlikely with the image – pull together your view of the person with the imagery you have created for the name. See this new compound image as vividly and really as possible. Don't concentrate on small bits of it, try for the whole.

Feedback The temptation is to break down the face into elements. In fact a well-known early book on using the mind more effectively recommends doing just this. Unfortunately, this doesn't fit well with the way the brain appears to store images of faces. It's fine to use an outstanding feature as a hook, but many people don't have one, and the feature should always be combined with the holistic image.

Outcome Being able to put a name to a face reliably and quickly is a very valuable skill, well worth the effort involved in familiarizing yourself with the technique.

Variations As practice helps, you could also try this before you get onto real people by taking a newspaper and looking for photographs of people you don't recognize. Use the technique to pin the name to the picture. It won't be quite as effective with a photograph, but it will give you some practice.

Knowledge	✪
Memory	✪✪✪✪
Creativity	✪
Fun	✪✪

5.56 The thrill factor

Preparation None.
Running time Five minutes.
Resources None.
Frequency Once.

Many of the exercises in this book look at building up skills and resources you need to improve your knowledge management and creativity, but there is one fundamental element of both of these that can't really be learnt. It's the thrill factor. If your area of knowledge – or the area you are trying to be creative in – thrills you, you will be better able to succeed.

There's a real problem here. It may be that you will never be able to get a thrill out of your work area, in which case, the only solution may be to change what you do. Drastic, yes, but effective.

For the moment, just spend a few minutes thinking about what it is that gives you that tingle of excitement. Take in as many different areas at once. Don't worry if they seem trivial – like playing with a new technical toy – get them down.

If you really want to encourage a build-up of knowledge and creativity, you will have to get more of these thrill factors into your work. Think about it.

Feedback This assumes that there are some things that thrill you. If you are cynical about everything, knowing that there is nothing of interest, nothing that can provide excitement, then you need to try to suspend that cynicism and find the thrill. It may not be easy, but it is possible.

Outcome We aren't accustomed to think about feelings in business, yet feelings can have a big impact on brain-related activities. Bringing a thrill into your work will make a very positive contribution.

Variations You can take a similar look at the tangential but not quite identical area of fun. What do you find fun? How can you incorporate fun elements in what you do? Fun is more strongly weighted towards creativity, where thrill balances knowledge and creativity.

Knowledge	✪✪✪✪
Memory	✪
Creativity	✪✪✪✪
Fun	✪✪✪

5.57 Different views

Preparation None.
Running time Five minutes.
Resources None.
Frequency Once.

Attempt an answer to all of these three short puzzles before moving on to the feedback.

- What is the result of adding 15 and 5 three times?
- A farmer was infuriated to see five rabbits eating his lettuces. He shot one rabbit – how many rabbits were left?
- Is there any way to drop an uncooked egg on to a concrete floor from 10 metres up without cracking it?

Feedback Don't go any further until you've attempted some sort of answer to each.Last chance to consider your answer. The answers are: 20 (it doesn't matter how many times you do it, you still get 20), none (the other four ran away), yes (it's actually very hard to crack a concrete floor using an uncooked egg). Each of these puzzles comes at the question from a different direction to the one you were expecting. Once you've groaned at the answers (if you hadn't already guessed them), take a minute to examine what was happening.

Outcome Creativity is all about seeing the world in a different way, or coming at a problem from a different direction. These puzzles work in exactly the same way. By practising this sort of puzzle, you have a much better chance of coming up with creative ideas. This is also an effective lesson for knowledge management. In each case, you knew the answer – it was the question you didn't understand. It emphasizes the need for careful questioning when you are acquiring knowledge.

Variations Get hold of a book of this sort of puzzle and practise the type of thinking required. You may also find cryptic crossword puzzles give the same kind of exercise.

Knowledge	✪✪✪
Memory	✪
Creativity	✪✪✪✪
Fun	✪✪✪

5.58 Binning paper

Preparation None.
Running time 10 minutes.
Resources Your files; notepad.
Frequency Once.

Look through your personal files and documents. Many of us keep copies of a huge range of information sources for future reference. We are not looking at books here, but magazines, journals, newspapers, cuttings, memos, papers, and so forth.

Make a note of the principal sources. Now see if there are ways you can dispose of these mountains of paper and move to a more accessible source of the same information. Is the journal, magazine or newspaper available on CD-ROM? If so, you will be able to find the information you need when you need it much quicker, without being surrounded by junk piles. Is the information you need available on-line? Are the memos or e-mails you have printed archived in an electronic form? As long as there is a secure, searchable repository you can dispose of your paper and find things more easily.

Feedback It can be quite a wrench to lose those piles of paper, but make sure you are hanging on to them for the right reason. Information can only contribute to knowledge if it is readily available and can be integrated with other sources. A five-foot stack of magazines has very limited chances of doing this effectively. Occasionally, there is a good reason for sticking to paper – for example, CD-ROM versions of magazines often don't include the advertising, and it may be that you need the advertising for something, but often you can compromise by combining the CD-ROM with the latest version of the magazine.

Outcome Getting rid of paper sounds a mundane, time management sort of activity, but the reason you stored this paper was to make it an active part of your knowledge base, and it can't do that if the information contained in it isn't readily accessible. Indexed electronic forms make this much more practical.

Variations Sometimes, it is worth scanning documents to include them in an electronic knowledge base, but beware of the magpie inclination – make sure the information is being collected for a reason.

Knowledge	✪✪✪✪
Memory	✪✪
Creativity	✪
Fun	✪✪

5.59 Something completely different

Preparation A problem or idea required.
Running time 10 minutes.
Resources None.
Frequency Once.

This is an approach to enhance your creativity that is best tried when you have a problem in mind or an idea you are working on. The activity is simple – do something completely different, unconnected with your problem for 10 minutes. This should involve an activity with lots of input, not simply sitting still, having a drink or chatting. While you are doing this different thing – it might be reading a book on a totally different subject, going for a walk, watching the TV – keep your problem in mind, even though you are really concentrating on what it is you are doing. Look for things in what you are doing that will provide inspiration with your problem. This might mean looking at what you are doing in quite a different way. At the end of the 10 minutes, return to your problem.

Feedback Note that this is very different approach to *Unconscious creativity*, 5.61. There you put the problem out of your mind and don't think about it. Here you are looking for positive inspiration in an unconnected field. This is one of the reasons this book emphasizes the value of reading – and reading a wide range of subjects – because the opportunities for sparking an idea are very significant. As a side benefit, you will come back to your thoughts refreshed by the change, but that isn't the main aim.

Outcome Many of the great ideas of the past have come from looking at something very different and drawing parallels. The mind is always using models and metaphors to hang ideas on: here we are fertilising this process.

Variations Don't always use the same distraction, although some will deliver again and again.

Knowledge	✪✪
Memory	✪
Creativity	✪✪✪✪
Fun	✪✪

5.60 Programmed thought

Preparation Get a video recorder manual.
Running time 10 minutes.
Resources Notepad.
Frequency Once.

Find the part of a video recorder manual that tells you how to set the timer and phrase the instructions as a set of rules. Limit yourself to these instructions:

```
IF (something is true)          WHILE (something is true)
THEN                            THEN
(do something)                  (do something)
END of IF                       END of WHILE
```

Put in the END line, so you can see where you have finished. You might like to use a programmer's trick of indenting. Move everything in the 'do something' section to the right, so it's obvious where it begins and ends. Feel free to include 'AND', 'BUT' and 'NOT' in your instructions. You can also extend IF with an alternative statement like OTHERWISE. So part of the result might be:

```
IF the video recorder is switched on
THEN
        Press the button to set a new record time
        [Other instructions for setting a new start time]
        IF there is a tape in the recorder AND it is blank
THEN
        Press the Timer button
        OTHERWISE
                [etc]
        END of IF
OTHERWISE
        Switch it on
        Start again
END of IF
```

Feedback Either ask someone else to check your rules, or leave them for a while then check them yourself. Have you taken into account every possibility (like putting in a blank tape)? Turning a task into rules shows how complex even a simple action can be – and why computer programs with millions of lines of code often include mistakes.

Outcome This is a good way of tackling a badly documented or complex procedure. It can help to identify holes in the procedure, but needs several reviews to ensure that there is a good correspondence with reality.

Variations Try this approach on any procedure or piece of knowledge involving action (even mental action like decision making). It is best applied to a non-trivial but well-contained area.

Knowledge	✪✪✪✪
Memory	✪
Creativity	✪
Fun	✪✪

5.61 Unconscious creativity

Preparation A problem or idea required.
Running time 10 minutes.
Resources None.
Frequency Once.

For this exercise you need a problem or an idea that you are working on. It needs to be fresh, rather than something you've been working on for days. If there isn't anything appropriate, use an artificial problem like, 'How to develop a new type of children's snack' or, 'How to cut down waiting time in accident and emergency departments'.

Spend five minutes thinking through the problem area. Positively avoid solutions. Just think about what the problem is, who is involved in it, what happens at the moment, and so on. Now put the problem to one side. Revisit it briefly (just the problem, not solutions) just before you go to sleep.

Come back to the problem after three or four days. Spend a minute thinking about it, then sit down with a piece of paper and write down what you could do. Don't analyse, just let whatever comes to mind flow out. If nothing comes after a few seconds, start to write anything at all without 'steering' the thoughts, then pull yourself gently back to the problem.

Feedback Sometimes this technique won't deliver, but surprisingly often partly-formed ideas will emerge. As Guy Claxton points out in *Hare Brain, Tortoise Mind* (see Chapter 6), we are capable of much more unconscious effort than we normally admit. Many creativity techniques involve taking the unconscious by surprise. This approach lets the unconscious take its own pace. It's not necessarily better, but makes a valuable alternative.

Outcome If you find this approach delivers, consider using it as an explicit technique, but the important thing is to allow time for unconscious connections to be made.

Variations You need to be able to let go of the problem consciously to let the unconscious deal with it – yet any important problem will nag at you. If you can use an electronic diary or task list to alert you in a few days time, your conscious mind will be more comfortable with letting go.

Knowledge	✪✪✪
Memory	✪
Creativity	✪✪✪✪
Fun	✪✪

5.62 Scribbling

Preparation None.
Running time 30 minutes.
Resources Notepad or word processor.
Frequency Once.

This exercise is simple to describe, harder to do. Write a short story. Try to cover an unusual topic – you might try science fiction or the sort of 'twist in the tale' story that Roald Dahl was so good at. Don't say, 'I can't write' or, 'it won't be any good'. You aren't entering the Booker Prize, this is an exercise in creativity.

The suggested time is 30 minutes – try to keep to this. You should be able to get an undisturbed 30 minutes somewhere in your schedule. Your output needn't be long. The creativity book *Imagination Engineering* (see page 107) features a short story by American writer Gene Wolfe that only runs to around 400 words – but it's no less effective because of that.

Feedback If you are having trouble starting, try *Story time*, 5.3, first to remind yourself what short stories are like. If a topic doesn't come to mind, take a couple of totally unrelated items – perhaps something you can see around you and something mentioned on the news – and bring them together in a strange situation. Why has it happened? What do the people involved feel? What will they do? Don't wait for inspiration – force yourself to start writing, however terrible you feel the output is.

Outcome Creative writing can be quite an unpleasant exercise, but there is no doubt that it stimulates your creative responses and will help you to tone up your creativity.

Variations If you've time to do the exercise twice, do it a second time in slightly different circumstances. Come up with a topic by putting a person from a work of fiction you enjoy into a dangerous situation in a favourite film. Spend a couple of minutes jotting down initial thoughts. Then leave it three or four days before you write it. The unconscious is a powerful tool for creativity – if you've got the time, it's worth adding it to your weaponry.

Knowledge	✪
Memory	✪
Creativity	✪✪✪✪
Fun	✪✪

5.63 Questioning everything

Preparation None.
Running time Five minutes.
Resources Trade magazine or technical book.
Frequency Once.

Take a copy of a trade journal or book that covers your own area of expertise. If you don't have anything appropriate, a factual newspaper story will do, but something in a specialist area of interest is best. Now spend five minutes assessing it. You aren't interested in the content directly. What you are looking for are assumptions. Assumptions that the writer makes. Assumptions you would normally make in reading the piece (for a book, take the first few pages of the second chapter).

What would happen if these assumptions weren't true? Would anything be different? How do you know they are true?

Feedback This is an exercise to expose your own way of thinking. We all make assumptions all the time. These assumptions can sometimes block the development of knowledge, and can certainly prevent creativity. If we had stuck with the assumption that the sun (and everything else) rotated round the earth, we would have been unable to make many other deductions in disciplines as far ranging as astrophysics and theology. Our ability to think creatively is always being undermined by assumptions that don't necessarily hold true.

Outcome Once you can spot the assumptions you and others are making, it becomes easier to do something about them. This doesn't mean always ignoring them, but you can then act in the conscious awareness of the assumptions you are making.

Variations Assumption spotting can be an entertaining game when listening to speeches (especially political speeches) and reading almost anything factual. Try it now and then to keep your assumption awareness in trim (it's a particularly good way of getting through a boring speech).

Knowledge	✪✪✪✪
Memory	✪
Creativity	✪✪✪✪
Fun	✪✪

5.64 Cloak and dagger

Preparation None.
Running time Five minutes.
Resources Notepad.
Frequency Once.

Imagine you had a small amount of text – a page of A4. You are in a small room which contains only a PC, a desk with three drawers and a bookcase. The bookcase has half a dozen thick reference books on it and a couple of filing boxes. How would you hide the text in such a way that it was retrievable by you, and on plain view, but not retrievable by someone else? You can use whatever tools you like to turn the text into a readily concealed form, provided the tools can be hidden away, too.

Feedback If you haven't spent a couple of minutes thinking of ways of achieving this goal, go back and do it before reading on. Try to be as creative as possible. I once needed a creative solution to this problem for a novel, and asked a hotshot computer programmer. He suggested using a picture on the PC. Pictures are stored in files which specify the colour of each dot (pixel) that makes up the picture. By using the least important bit of data for each dot, you can store a lot of information without making an obvious difference to the picture. Of course, you would need appropriate software to accomplish this, but that's just a tool. Interestingly, since then, a software company has started selling such a piece of software. This isn't the only solution, nor the most creative – it's just one example.

Outcome It might seem that thinking out the answer to such an unlikely problem won't help everyday creativity, but the processes involved are perfect for strengthening the creative ability.

Variations The advantage of this type of exercise is that you can think up your own with very little effort. Just put together a near-impossible requirement (anything from a 'locked room' murder mystery to an automatic shoelace tier), and spend a couple of minutes working on solutions.

Knowledge	✪✪
Memory	✪
Creativity	✪✪✪✪
Fun	✪✪✪

5.65 On the level

Preparation None.
Running time Five minutes.
Resources Notepad.
Frequency Once.

This exercise uses a powerful creativity technique called the level chain. Usually this is a vehicle for developing specific new ideas – here we are simply going to stretch your creative thinking.

The level chain works by taking an object or idea and setting up a chain of associated objects, each more specific (down a level) or less specific (up a level) than the original. The chain moves randomly. For example, one might go:

Piggy Bank (up to) Container (down to) Bottle (down to) Blue bottle (up to) Pest

Note how the last link in the chain cheats, using the common name for a blowfly, a bluebottle – that's fine. In a conventional level chain, we might be looking for a new financial product and would stop when the chain suggested one. Now try a few chains yourself. Start with a specific object. Randomly move up and down the levels. Make your chain at least five items long.

Do two or three chains without any particular aim in mind. Finally, think of the target of a great new invention. Pick an ordinary household item and do a few level chains, aiming to derive a great new invention. It doesn't have to be exactly what comes in the chain – for example, using the chain above, blue bottle might make me think of a bottle that I can put things in to turn them blue, or a device that flies around the house looking for germs and eliminating them.

Feedback Don't worry if you don't come up with something specific, it's the exercise that counts.

Outcome The level chain is a great way of freeing up the connections in your brain so you can put together new concepts. The more you use it, the easier it becomes to make the leap without even using the technique.

Variations I've labelled this as a one-off, but it can be repeated to taste – and of course, can be used for actual generation of ideas as well as enhancing your creativity.

Knowledge	✪
Memory	✪
Creativity	✪✪✪✪
Fun	✪✪

5.66 Go gallery

Preparation Find an art gallery displaying modern art.
Running time 30 minutes.
Resources None.
Frequency Once.

This is a very simple exercise. Find an art gallery displaying modern art. Go and visit it. Spend half an hour wandering round looking at the exhibits. That's it.

Well, almost. When you are looking around, take a rather different approach to the usual gallery visitor. Look at each painting, or sculpture or installation in turn. Don't spend a long time – perhaps 30 seconds or a minute for each. In that time, do one thing only. Consider what the artwork makes you think of. Don't worry if the piece is a load of rubbish that you wouldn't give houseroom to – that's not the point. Just let the inspirations flow.

Feedback If you are the sort of person who hasn't time for modern art (or art in general), don't give this one a miss – it is particularly suitable for you. You have to be able to suspend your normal irritation that 'so-called art', which could have been done by a chimpanzee, commands huge prices. All you are doing is using the art as a launchpad for your own thoughts and ideas.

Outcome There's a double benefit from this one. Just getting out of your normal habitat can help to enhance your creativity, but using the works of art as provocation for different ways of thinking can be very valuable.

Variations If you haven't got easy access to a gallery, get hold of one of the excellent CD-ROMs of art or find something appropriate on the World Wide Web. As an alternative, a scrap yard or any site of urban or industrial decay can be equally effective. In fact, come to think of it, they're probably more artistic, too.

Knowledge	✪✪
Memory	✪
Creativity	✪✪✪✪
Fun	✪✪

5.67 Strengthening your ghosts

Preparation None.
Running time 10 minutes.
Resources Quiet environment.
Frequency Several times.

Sit quietly and comfortably with your eyes closed. Imagine yourself in an environment you know well. The office, a friend's house, the pub – anywhere as long as it isn't your current location. Try to build up a detailed picture of the location as you see it when you approach. The doors, the windows, the colour scheme. Walk up to the door. Imagine its detail – what is the door furniture like? Open the door – what does the handle feel like? Now go inside. Try to bring back as much as possible of your surroundings. What is the floor like? The walls?

Once you are inside, wander around. Interact with items you can remember in the environment. Don't just consider visual aspects. What do they feel like? What sounds are there? What smells?

Feedback Having a so-called photographic memory depends on the ability to capture and revisit images. While this can't be learnt to the extent of bringing back a whole page of a book at a time, we can all improve our imagery and ability to remember. Notice the strong dependence on the senses, a common theme when looking at memory and knowledge.

Outcome By undertaking this type of exercise you can enhance your ability to remember things that have just been seen more clearly. This is an ability we all have to a considerable degree, but generally it is pushed out of the way by the development of the conscious mind. Visualization also helps with your building of models and metaphors, essential for knowledge management and creativity.

Variations This is an exercise that benefits from several attempts. Try different locations. When the approach is working well for you, start making the imagery more creative. Imagine going somewhere you haven't been, or couldn't go (like into the core of a nuclear power station). Don't restrict yourself any more to the limitations of physics – if you want to fly, fly.

Knowledge	✪✪✪
Memory	✪✪✪✪
Creativity	✪✪✪
Fun	✪✪

5.68 School daze

Preparation None.
Running time Five minutes.
Resources None.
Frequency Once.

Another problem to challenge your thinking skills.

I normally drive over to pick up my daughter from school at 4pm. One day, she is let out of school one hour early and decides to walk back, meeting me on the way. We get back home 10 minutes earlier than normal. If I always drive at the same speed, and left home at just the right time to pick her up at 4pm, which of the following pieces of information would you need to determine how long she had been walking (you can choose more than one): her walking speed, my driving speed, the distance from home to school.

Feedback If you haven't already got an answer, try to jot one down now. Don't read any further. Last chance to consider your answer. There was an element of sleight of hand here. The answer is none of them: you already have enough information. As we got back 10 minutes earlier than normal, I met her five minutes earlier than normal (trimming five minutes off outbound and inbound journeys), so she spent 55 minutes walking.

Outcome Often you will have too much information. Trimming out the unnecessary, or the search for the unnecessary, is a vital part of knowledge management.

Variations Consider occasions when you have chased unnecessary information. Are there ways of making information gathering 'just in time' so that it doesn't take unnecessary effort and conceal the knowledge?

Knowledge	✪✪✪✪
Memory	✪
Creativity	✪✪✪
Fun	✪✪✪

5.69 Context is everything

Preparation None.
Running time Five minutes.
Resources None.
Frequency Oncc.

We've all been in the circumstance where you know that you know something, but can't quite put your finger on it. It might be a telephone number, an address, a scientific formula or the name of a company. Your natural inclination may well be to remove all distractions to try to bring something back. But this isn't the best approach.

For the purposes of this exercise, make up something you need to remember. But don't go about it the usual way. First think what you know surrounding the thing you need to remember. If it's practical, in the next few minutes experience as many as you can of the sensations that you might associate with the memory. The sights, the sounds, the smells – even the touch and motion. If that isn't practical, get out of your chair, move around a little, then sit back down and try to bring to mind those sights, sounds, smells and other feelings. Often this will result in the memory being retrieved.

Feedback Research in the laboratory has shown that memory fails much more often without the right context to hang it on. It might seem common sense that the best way to remember things would be to have as little stimulus as possible – to be in a controlled environment with nothing impacting on your senses – but the reality seems quite different. This is not arguing for permanently disruptive surroundings. Distraction is no help when you are trying to concentrate. But when you need to remember something that is eluding you, make use of your knowledge of the way memory works. Don't sit in isolation. Give your memory a chance by indulging in the right kind of stimulation.

Outcome Sometimes the way that memory works is counter-intuitive. We are so used to the idea that distractions are bad, that we forget the benefits of context. Remember this... next time you need to remember something.

Variations If you have something real you need to remember, so much the better – the point of the exercise, though, is to establish the principle.

Knowledge	✪✪✪
Memory	✪✪✪✪
Creativity	✪✪
Fun	✪✪

5.70 Take a letter

Preparation Some long numbers to remember.
Running time 10 minutes.
Resources Notepad.
Frequency Several times.

In this technique, each number is assigned a number of letters. You then make up a word or sentence out of the number you want to remember, adding vowels to pad it out, and associate that with the context. In the list below, a key letter is associated with the number and other sound-alikes are included.

1 – t (th, d) – a single, strong downstroke
2 – n – two downstrokes
3 – m – three downstrokes
4 – r – last letter of the number four
5 – l – roman numeral 50
6 – j (ch, sh) – j is 6 backwards (sort of)
7 – k (hard g, ng, qu) – k (with a back flick at the top) is like a 7 with another inverted one attached
8 – f (v) – a fancy written lower case f can be like 8
9 – p (b) – 9 is a mirror image of p
0 – z (s) – start of zero

Spend about five minutes memorizing the letter patterns, then try some basic numbers. You will need to come back to this a few times to fix the letter patterns in your memory.

Feedback This technique takes longer to learn than a basic technique like *Number shapes*, 5.51, but it is more flexible when dealing with long numbers or lists of numbers. The trouble with the technique is that it does take quite an effort to remember the letters used to represent the numbers – but that effort will be well rewarded.

Outcome This is a great way of learning telephone numbers, physical constants and other irritatingly long numbers.

Variations You can devise your own series of letter/number combinations, but the one shown here has proved effective, and variants have now been in use for several hundred years.

Knowledge	✪✪
Memory	✪✪✪✪
Creativity	✪✪
Fun	✪✪

5.71 Get another life

Preparation Get hold of a business biography book.
Running time 15 minutes.
Resources Book.
Frequency Several times a year.

Elsewhere (*Get a laugh*, 5.37), I've recommended business humour as a source of creativity. Another particularly effective inspiration for business creativity is the business biography. The combination of the development of extraordinary businesses with some very strange personalities makes for an exploration of a very different view on life. The aim here isn't to turn you into another Bill Gates, but rather to help to see the business world in a different way. Spend about quarter of an hour reading a section from one of these books. Try to do this on a regular basis – you may well find you need to finish the book once you've started: don't fight it.

Feedback Reading in the workplace is frowned on, even when the subject is serious business texts, so doing this in working hours may not be a good move. It ought to be – after all, this is probably more educational than many of the courses you may have attended, but the fact is that it is not an acceptable thing to do. That being the case, take the pragmatic view and read it in your lunchtime, or out of business hours.

Outcome Business biographies are a particularly effective aid to business creativity because they are readable (being dull is simply a turn-off for creativity), and they push you into a different way of thinking – often incorporating a new sort of energy that just isn't present in your own business life. Recommended.

Variations For specifics on finding business biographies, see Chapter 6.

Knowledge	✪✪✪
Memory	✪
Creativity	✪✪✪✪
Fun	✪✪✪✪

5.72 An excellent mistake

Preparation None.
Running time 10 minutes.
Resources Notepad.
Frequency Once.

Think back over the last few weeks. Work backwards until you hit something that really went wrong. Having your diary to hand might help to spot where it happened. Spend a couple of minutes thinking about what happened. What led up to the error? What was happening around it? What could you learn from it for the future?

Feedback Learning from mistakes is a crucial part of building knowledge and gaining creativity. If you are going to be creative, you will make mistakes. If you want to foster expertise, you will get things wrong along the way. Unfortunately, our culture (and especially our business culture) is not very positive about mistakes. Everything from Total Quality Management to the culture of taking the blame suggests that mistakes are wholly bad. But to keep on developing we need to be able accept mistakes, drop everything and start again in a different direction without feeling negative, and learn from the experience.

Outcome By making learning from your mistakes a natural course, you can build up your expertise and make more effective use of your creativity.

Variations Consider having a horror log, where you record things that go wrong, and enter some simple lessons for each mistake. This doesn't have to be a full-blown postmortem, you can do it in a few minutes. Where there's a significant cock-up and you manage to turn things round quickly and effectively, consider a celebration of the disaster. Celebrating failures that you have learnt from can be beneficial.

Knowledge	✪✪✪✪
Memory	✪
Creativity	✪✪✪✪
Fun	✪✪

5.73 Using it

Preparation The other exercises.
Running time Indefinite.
Resources Notepad.
Frequency Regularly.

This exercise is the simplest and the hardest in the whole book. When you have done some (if not all) of the exercises from this chapter, start to use them in everyday life. Don't just think, 'That's interesting' and go back to your old ways, do something, and keep on doing something.

To an extent you won't have any choice. The exercises to enhance your creativity will be subtly changing your way of thinking already, but you need to keep up the approach of looking at things differently. Check out some of the reading suggestions in Chapter 6 to find other ways of working on your creativity.

The memory techniques are much more down to you doing something with them. Don't give in to laziness and think, 'I won't bother today' – next time you meet a group of people, remember their names. Next time you go shopping, memorize the list. Make the techniques a part of your day-to-day life.

The techniques that focus most on knowledge sit somewhere between the two. There will be some basic changes already, but you will also have new tools for retrieving and structuring information, new ways of looking at your knowledge base. Again, the essential thing is to keep it up.

Feedback This is an exercise particularly suited to people who like reading a book from end to end. The final exercise was originally *An excellent mistake*, 5.72, but that seemed a bit of a depressing way to finish (it isn't really depressing, but the F word can give that impression). Congratulations on getting here – now get on with using your new skills.

Outcome There are few skills that give more benefit with less effort than brainpower skills, yet most of us have a natural reluctance to use them. Be aware of this. The star ratings for this exercise are all potential ones (so you won't find them in the tables in the Appendix). You can make it anything from zero to four. Go for four.

Variations None.

Knowledge	✪✪✪✪
Memory	✪✪✪✪
Creativity	✪✪✪✪
Fun	✪✪✪✪

5

OTHER SOURCES

MORE BRAIN DEVELOPMENT

Instant Brainpower gives a great start to your brain-building course, but you might like to look elsewhere, either to work on specific aspects of brain-building or to simply continue your all-round development. These sources will help with further support.

WEB SOURCES

The World Wide Web has become the universal source for assistance and information. In part, it will be a source of information to support your knowledge and creativity. It can also help with more information on brainpower. To find more general information, input 'brainpower' or 'brain skills' into a search engine or Web index and browse around. Here are a couple of the best-known addresses to get you started:

AltaVista – **http://www.altavista.com**
Yahoo! – **http://www.yahoo.com**

BOOKS

Many of the books below are available from high street bookshops, but check the Creativity Unleashed on-line bookshop at **http://www.cul.co.uk/books** which provides plenty of information and has direct buying links to the biggest on-line bookshops in the US and the UK. It has specific references for creativity, general business, humorous business and business biographies. If you are trying to expand your fictional input, it also has references for the two most creativity-stimulating fiction genres: science fiction and crime. It's also worth checking there for more up-to-date references, and for books that are hard to get hold of in the UK.

GENERAL

Brian Clegg (1998) *The Chameleon Manager*, Butterworth Heinemann
This book looks at the new skills needed to manage your life and work as we move into the 21st century. These come down to creativity, communication and knowledge. *The Chameleon Manager* looks at changing to work the way you want to work, to make the most out of your life, providing an excellent complement to *Instant Brainpower*.

Guy Claxton (1997) *Hare Brain, Tortoise Mind*, Fourth Estate
Sometimes working on a problem in a determined, methodical way doesn't work. Sometimes it's even detrimental to the result. This book considers the approach that is often ignored by Western culture of letting a problem or an idea slosh about in the unconscious for a while to help the brain to sort it out. Claxton argues, with much scientific evidence, that this approach is much better for fuzzy, complex decisions.

Peter Russell (1979) The *Brain Book*, Routledge and Kegan Paul
A good introduction to the brain and how to use it better. Goes into a lot of detail on how the brain works (or might work), then looks at the practicalities of improving your brain skills.

KNOWLEDGE MANAGEMENT

Tony Buzan (1982) *Use Your Head*, BBC Books
Some overlaps with *The Mind Map Book* in the next section, but *Use Your Head* provides guidance on a wider range of skills, such as speed reading and learning, which are particularly relevant to knowledge management.

Brian Clegg (1999) *Mining the Internet*, Kogan Page
If you aren't going to be an information magpie, you need to be able quickly to haul in information when you need it to expand or revise your knowledge. This is a practical guide to the skills needed to use Internet (including the World Wide Web) as a knowledge source, and to find the right information in the minimum of time.

Mariana Funes and Nancy Johnson (1998) *Honing Your Knowledge Skills*, Butterworth Heinemann
Combines some detailed techniques for expanding your knowledge management skills with a lot of the theory underlying it. Particularly valuable if you are contemplating a career in knowledge management.

MEMORY

Tony and Barry Buzan (1993) *The Mind Map Book*, BBC Books
A beautifully illustrated guide to the use of mind maps to take notes, structure ideas and aid memory. Written by Tony Buzan, the developer of the mind map concept, with his brother.

CREATIVITY

Edward de Bono (1996) *Serious Creativity*, HarperCollins
A wide-ranging book from the best-known UK creativity guru. De Bono invented the term 'lateral thinking' and here he explores the benefits of creativity and describes his personally preferred techniques. Quite a dry book, but pulls together all de Bono's key work on the subject.

Brian Clegg (1999) *Creativity and Innovation for Managers*, Butterworth Heinemann
An overview for the busy manager, showing the need for creativity, where it came from as a management discipline, how it is applied, and how to make it work in a company. Puts creativity alongside other business techniques, and provides an agenda for introducing corporate innovation.

Brain Clegg and Paul Birch (1996) *Imagination Engineering*, Pitman Publishing
A toolkit for business creativity, providing a practical but enjoyable guide to making creativity work. Introduces a four stage process for business creativity, equally applicable for a five minute session or a week concentrating on a single problem. Plenty of depth, but fun, too.

Brian Clegg and Paul Birch (1999) *Instant Creativity*, Kogan Page
Companion to this book in the Kogan Page *Instant* series, *Instant Creativity* applies the same quick-to-use approach of an introduction followed by 70+ practical techniques for solving problems and generating new ideas.

Brian Clegg and Paul Birch (1998) *Instant Teamwork*, Kogan Page
Another member of the Kogan Page *Instant* series, *Instant Teamwork* looks at encouraging creativity from a team viewpoint with a whole range of techniques for breaking down barriers, increasing energy and getting a team working in a more creative fashion.

Betty Edwards (1986) *Drawing on the Right Side of Your Brian*, Collins
Betty Edwards looks at why most of us 'can't draw' and provides specific techniques both to help you to draw and to help you to see what your subject really is, improving visualization skills.

Roger von Oech (1983) *A Whack on the Side of the Head*, Warner Books
In total contrast to de Bono, von Oech's laid-back Californian style attacks the blockers to creativity in an enjoyable way. Sometimes feels more like a humour book than a management text, but none the worse for this, and there's a serious message under the gloss.

HUMOUR

Scott Adams (1997) *The Dilbert Future*, HarperCollins, 1997
Classic Dilbert cartoons, featuring the hapless hero whose software engineering in a goldfish bowl of a cubicle is always under threat from colleagues, the boss and the environment. A double treat, as Adams also parodies some well-known business books, putting across a very practical message. For more Dilbert, see the Creativity Unleashed Web site **http://www.cul.co.uk/books**.

Robert Townsend (1985) *Further Up the Organization*, Coronet
Townsend's experience, as a director of American Express and President and Chairman of Avis, allows him to view the realities of business through experience rather than the theory of the business school. In a series of short, readable articles he pulls apart much conventional business thinking.

BUSINESS BIOGRAPHIES

Michael Leapman (1987) T*he Last Days of the Beeb*, Coronet
A fascinating study of the Byzantine, bizarre organization that was the BBC before recent reorganizations ripped it apart and put it together in a different form. There's nothing like an account of a disaster for putting across some very significant lessons.

James Wallace and Jim Erickson (1992) *Hard Drive*, John Wiley & Sons
Wallace and Erickson penetrate the myth behind the founding and growth of Microsoft and the life of Bill Gates. This sort of business biography is a great source of creativity, because it looks at a very different approach to life and business to that experienced by most of us.

Just a sample of the many impressive business biographies around these days. The Creativity Unleashed Web site **http://www.cul.co.uk/books** has recommendations of many more.

APPENDIX: THE SELECTOR

THE RANDOM SELECTOR

Take a watch with a second hand and note the number the second hand is pointing at now. Take that number technique from the list of 60 below.

No.	Ref.	Title
1	5.2	Water into wine
2	5.4	Category magic
3	5.5	Doing and knowing
4	5.6	Metaphorically speaking
5	5.7	Sense and sensibility
6	5.8	Altered states
7	5.9	All that glisters
8	5.11	Extremes
9	5.12	Surveying your mind
10	5.13	Story chains
11	5.14	Muddled model
12	5.17	Words of wisdom
13	5.18	Round the world
14	5.19	Name game
15	5.20	Holistic awareness
16	5.21	Pub quiz
17	5.22	Number rhymes
18	5.23	No time to read
19	5.24	Spinning knowledge
20	5.25	Going down
21	5.27	We ask the questions
22	5.28	Follow the finger
23	5.29	On the edge
24	5.30	Quick on the draw
25	5.31	Story time
26	5.32	Leaf mould
27	5.33	Car and goats
28	5.34	Found story
29	5.35	Remember, remember
30	5.36	Life saver
31	5.37	Get a laugh

No.	Ref.	Title
32	5.38	Rapt concentration
33	5.39	Material gains
34	5.40	Twisters
35	5.42	Fact quest
36	5.43	Versatile coat hangers
37	5.44	Game theory
38	5.45	Technical creativity
39	5.46	Stolen thoughts
40	5.49	Birthday bonanza
41	5.50	Critical judgement
42	5.51	Number shapes
43	5.52	Encyclopedia dip
44	5.53	Horse whispers
45	5.54	Speed read
46	5.56	The thrill factor
47	5.57	Different views
48	5.58	Binning paper
49	5.59	Something completely different
50	5.60	Programmed thought
51	5.62	Scribbling
52	5.63	Questioning everything
53	5.64	Cloak and dagger
54	5.65	On the level
55	5.66	Go gallery
56	5.67	Strengthening your ghosts
57	5.68	School daze
58	5.69	Context is everything
59	5.70	Take a letter
60	5.72	An excellent mistake

TECHNIQUES IN TIMING ORDER

This table sorts the techniques by the suggested timings. Those at the top take the longest, those towards the bottom are the quickest.

Ref.	**Title**
30 Minutes	
5.1	On the box
5.31	Story time
5.44	Game theory
5.48	Bookshop raid
5.62	Scribbling
5.66	Go gallery
15 Minutes	
5.37	Get a laugh
5.71	Get another life
10 Minutes	
5.4	Category magic
5.7	Sense and sensibility
5.8	Altered states
5.12	Surveying your mind
5.20	Holistic awareness
5.24	Spinning knowledge
5.27	We ask the questions
5.28	Follow the finger
5.29	On the edge
5.30	Quick on the draw
5.33	Car and goats
5.34	Found story
5.41	Mapping for memory
5.42	Fact quest
5.45	Technical creativity
5.46	Stolen thoughts
5.50	Critical judgement
5.51	Number shapes
5.52	Encyclopedia dip
5.58	Binning paper
5.59	Something completely different
5.60	Programmed thought
5.61	Unconscious creativity
5.67	Strengthening your ghosts
5.70	Take a letter
5.72	An excellent mistake

Ref.	**Title**
5 Minutes	
5.2	Water into wine
5.3	Broken record
5.5	Doing and knowing
5.6	Metaphorically speaking
5.9	All that glisters
5.10	Chunks and breaks
5.11	Extremes
5.13	Story chains
5.14	Muddled model
5.15	One more time
5.16	Take a note
5.17	Words of wisdom
5.18	Round the world
5.19	Name game
5.21	Pub quiz
5.22	Number rhymes
5.23	No time to read
5.25	Going down
5.26	The little black book
5.32	Leaf mould
5.35	Remember, remember
5.36	Life saver
5.38	Rapt concentration
5.39	Material gains
5.40	Twisters
5.43	Versatile coat hangers
5.47	Broken CD
5.49	Birthday bonanza
5.53	Horse whispers
5.54	Speed read
5.55	I never forget a face
5.56	The thrill factor
5.57	Different views
5.63	Questioning everything
5.64	Cloak and dagger
5.65	On the level
5.68	School daze
5.69	Context is everything

TECHNIQUES IN FREQUENCY ORDER

This table sorts the techniques by the frequency order. Those at the top are undertaken most frequently, those at the bottom once only.

Ref.	Title
Weekly	
5.26	The little black book
5.52	Encyclopedia dip
Regularly	
5.12	Surveying your mind
5.15	One more time
5.17	Words of wisdom
5.29	On the edge
Several times a year	
5.37	Get a laugh
5.71	Get another life
Several times	
5.6	Metaphorically speaking
5.13	Story chains
5.38	Rapt concentration
5.44	Game theory
5.54	Speed read
5.67	Strengthening your ghosts
5.70	Take a letter
Three times	
5.22	Number rhymes
5.51	Number shapes
Once	
5.1	On the box
5.2	Water into wine
5.3	Broken record
5.4	Category magic
5.5	Doing and knowing
5.7	Sense and sensibility
5.8	Altered states
5.9	All that glisters
5.10	Chunks and breaks
5.11	Extremes
5.14	Muddled model
5.16	Take a note
5.18	Round the world
5.19	Name game
5.20	Holistic awareness
5.21	Pub quiz
5.23	No time to read
5.24	Spinning knowledge
5.25	Going down
5.27	We ask the questions
5.28	Follow the finger
5.30	Quick on the draw
5.31	Story time
5.32	Leaf mould
5.33	Car and goats
5.34	Found story
5.35	Remember, remember
5.36	Life saver
5.39	Material gains
5.40	Twisters
5.41	Mapping for memory
5.42	Fact quest
5.43	Versatile coat hangers
5.45	Technical creativity
5.46	Stolen thoughts
5.47	Broken CD
5.48	Bookshop raid
5.49	Birthday bonanza
5.50	Critical judgement
5.53	Horse whispers
5.55	I never forget a face
5.56	The thrill factor
5.57	Different views
5.58	Binning paper
5.59	Something completely different
5.60	Programmed thought
5.61	Unconscious creativity
5.62	Scribbling
5.63	Questioning everything
5.64	Cloak and dagger
5.65	On the level
5.66	Go gallery
5.68	School daze
5.69	Context is everything
5.72	An excellent mistake

TECHNIQUES IN KNOWLEDGE ORDER

This table sorts the techniques by the knowledge star ratings attached to each. Those at the top have the highest star rating, those at the bottom the lowest.

✪✪✪✪

Ref.	Title
5.1	On the box
5.2	Water into wine
5.3	Broken record
5.4	Category magic
5.5	Doing and knowing
5.6	Metaphorically speaking
5.7	Sense and sensibility
5.9	All that glisters
5.17	Words of wisdom
5.20	Holistic awareness
5.23	No time to read
5.24	Spinning knowledge
5.26	The little black book
5.27	We ask the questions
5.28	Follow the finger
5.29	On the edge
5.32	Leaf mould
5.42	Fact quest
5.44	Game theory
5.46	Stolen thoughts
5.47	Broken CD
5.48	Bookshop raid
5.50	Critical judgement
5.52	Encyclopedia dip
5.54	Speed read
5.56	The thrill factor
5.58	Binning paper
5.60	Programmed thought
5.63	Questioning everything
5.68	School daze
5.72	An excellent mistake

✪✪✪

Ref.	Title
5.8	Altered states
5.10	Chunks and breaks
5.11	Extremes
5.12	Surveying your mind
5.15	One more time
5.16	Take a note
5.21	Pub quiz
5.25	Going down
5.30	Quick on the draw
5.36	Life saver
5.37	Get a laugh
5.40	Twisters
5.41	Mapping for memory
5.49	Birthday bonanza
5.57	Different views
5.61	Unconscious creativity
5.67	Strengthening your ghosts
5.69	Context is everything
5.71	Get another life

✪✪

Ref.	Title
5.13	Story chains
5.18	Round the world
5.22	Number rhymes
5.33	Car and goats
5.34	Found story
5.35	Remember, remember
5.38	Rapt concentration
5.39	Material gains
5.43	Versatile coat hangers
5.45	Technical creativity
5.51	Number shapes
5.53	Horse whispers
5.59	Something completely different
5.64	Cloak and dagger
5.66	Go gallery
5.70	Take a letter

✪

Ref.	Title
5.14	Muddled model
5.19	Name game
5.31	Story time
5.55	I never forget a face
5.62	Scribbling
5.65	On the level

TECHNIQUES IN MEMORY ORDER

This table sorts the techniques by the memory star ratings attached to each. Those at the top have the highest star rating, those at the bottom the lowest.

Ref.	Title
✪✪✪✪	
5.10	Chunks and breaks
5.11	Extremes
5.12	Surveying your mind
5.13	Story chains
5.15	One more time
5.19	Name game
5.22	Number rhymes
5.35	Remember, remember
5.41	Mapping for memory
5.51	Number shapes
5.55	I never forget a face
5.67	Strengthening your ghosts
5.69	Context is everything
5.70	Take a letter
✪✪✪	
5.4	Category magic
5.6	Metaphorically speaking
5.8	Altered states
5.16	Take a note
5.20	Holistic awareness
5.29	On the edge
5.38	Rapt concentration
✪✪	
5.7	Sense and sensibility
5.9	All that glisters
5.25	Going down
5.44	Game theory
5.58	Binning paper
✪	
5.1	On the box
5.2	Water into wine
5.3	Broken record
5.5	Doing and knowing
5.14	Muddled model
5.17	Words of wisdom
5.18	Round the world

Ref.	Title
5.21	Pub quiz
5.23	No time to read
5.24	Spinning knowledge
5.26	The little black book
5.27	We ask the questions
5.28	Follow the finger
5.30	Quick on the draw
5.31	Story time
5.32	Leaf mould
5.33	Car and goats
5.34	Found story
5.36	Life saver
5.37	Get a laugh
5.39	Material gains
5.40	Twisters
5.42	Fact quest
5.43	Versatile coat hangers
5.45	Technical creativity
5.46	Stolen thoughts
5.47	Broken CD
5.48	Bookshop raid
5.49	Birthday bonanza
5.50	Critical judgement
5.52	Encyclopedia dip
5.53	Horse whispers
5.54	Speed read
5.56	The thrill factor
5.57	Different views
5.59	Something completely different
5.60	Programmed thought
5.61	Unconscious creativity
5.62	Scribbling
5.63	Questioning everything
5.64	Cloak and dagger
5.65	On the level
5.66	Go gallery
5.68	School daze
5.71	Get another life
5.72	An excellent mistake

TECHNIQUES IN CREATIVITY ORDER

This table sorts the techniques by the creativity star ratings attached to each. Those at the top have the highest star rating, those at the bottom the lowest.

Ref.	Title
✪✪✪✪	
5.2	Water into wine
5.6	Metaphorically speaking
5.14	Muddled model
5.16	Take a note
5.18	Round the world
5.23	No time to read
5.25	Going down
5.30	Quick on the draw
5.31	Story time
5.32	Leaf mould
5.33	Car and goats
5.34	Found story
5.36	Life saver
5.37	Get a laugh
5.39	Material gains
5.40	Twisters
5.43	Versatile coat hangers
5.44	Game theory
5.45	Technical creativity
5.46	Stolen thoughts
5.49	Birthday bonanza
5.52	Encyclopedia dip
5.53	Horse whispers
5.56	The thrill factor
5.57	Different views
5.59	Something completely different
5.61	Unconscious creativity
5.62	Scribbling
5.63	Questioning everything
5.64	Cloak and dagger
5.65	On the level
5.66	Go gallery
5.71	Get another life
5.72	An excellent mistake
✪✪✪	
5.8	Altered states
5.11	Extremes
5.12	Surveying your mind
5.17	Words of wisdom
5.21	Pub quiz
5.38	Rapt concentration
5.50	Critical judgement
5.67	Strengthening your ghosts
5.68	School daze
✪✪	
5.10	Chunks and breaks
5.20	Holistic awareness
5.22	Number rhymes
5.24	Spinning knowledge
5.27	We ask the questions
5.28	Follow the finger
5.41	Mapping for memory
5.42	Fact quest
5.48	Bookshop raid
5.51	Number shapes
5.69	Context is everything
5.70	Take a letter
✪	
5.1	On the box
5.3	Broken record
5.4	Category magic
5.5	Doing and knowing
5.7	Sense and sensibility
5.9	All that glisters
5.13	Story chains
5.15	One more time
5.19	Name game
5.26	The little black book
5.29	On the edge
5.35	Remember, remember
5.47	Broken CD
5.54	Speed read
5.55	I never forget a face
5.58	Binning paper
5.60	Programmed thought

TECHNIQUES IN FUN ORDER

This table sorts the techniques by the fun star ratings attached to each. Those at the top have the highest star rating, those at the bottom the lowest.

Ref.	Title
✪✪✪✪	
5.23	No time to read
5.31	Story time
5.37	Get a laugh
5.39	Material gains
5.44	Game theory
5.71	Get another life
✪✪✪	
5.2	Water into wine
5.6	Metaphorically speaking
5.11	Extremes
5.13	Story chains
5.18	Round the world
5.21	Pub quiz
5.22	Number rhymes
5.25	Going down
5.32	Leaf mould
5.33	Car and goats
5.34	Found story
5.36	Life saver
5.40	Twisters
5.42	Fact quest
5.43	Versatile coat hangers
5.48	Bookshop raid
5.49	Birthday bonanza
5.52	Encyclopedia dip
5.53	Horse whispers
5.56	The thrill factor
5.57	Different views
5.64	Cloak and dagger
5.68	School daze
✪✪	
5.1	On the box
5.3	Broken record
5.5	Doing and knowing
5.7	Sense and sensibility
5.8	Altered states
5.9	All that glisters
5.10	Chunks and breaks
5.12	Surveying your mind
5.14	Muddled model
5.16	Take a note
5.17	Words of wisdom
5.19	Name game
5.20	Holistic awareness
5.24	Spinning knowledge
5.27	We ask the questions
5.29	On the edge
5.30	Quick on the draw
5.35	Remember, remember
5.38	Rapt concentration
5.41	Mapping for memory
5.45	Technical creativity
5.46	Stolen thoughts
5.47	Broken CD
5.50	Critical judgement
5.51	Number shapes
5.55	I never forget a face
5.58	Binning paper
5.59	Something completely different
5.60	Programmed thought
5.61	Unconscious creativity
5.62	Scribbling
5.63	Questioning everything
5.65	On the level
5.66	Go gallery
5.67	Strengthening your ghosts
5.69	Context is everything
5.70	Take a letter
5.72	An excellent mistake
✪	
5.4	Category magic
5.15	One more time
5.26	The little black book
5.28	Follow the finger
5.54	Speed read